Introduction

Over the past few months, I have had the honor and privilege of collecting the fresh inspiration posted by my mother, Piper Lumsden, on her Facebook page. She has been an incredible source of encouragement and hope to many people through the social media site, and now it has been compiled in a simple day-by-day calendar for you to read. Whether you study this as a devotional with your family, small group, or even by yourself, I am sure that you will find applicable encouragement for your daily life within these pages. I pray this book blesses you as you read it just as it did while I was editing and publishing it. God bless.

-Destiny Lumsden

Destiny Come Forth

January 1

PRAYER:

MAY YOU RISE ABOVE THE STORM

MAY YOU KEEP YOUR HOPES HIGH

MAY YOU SEE THE BIG PICTURE

MAY YOU SHARE GOD'S POINT OF VIEW

MAY YOU FLY HIGH BUT STAY GROUNDED

AMEN

DECREE:

YOU PUSH THROUGH THE DEBRI

YOU ARE UNSTOPPABLE

YOU REST WHEN NEEDED

YOU STAY HEALTHY

YOU ARE MORE THAN A CONQUEROR

FACT:

FASTING CLEARS THE WAY

INSPIRATION:

GET STRATEGIC

Destiny Come Forth

January 2

PRAYER:

MAY YOU PRESS INTO GOD

MAY YOU STAY FOCUSSED

MAY YOU FEEL THE LOVE

MAY YOU SHARE HIS LOVE

MAY YOU KEEP MOVING FORWARD

AMEN

DECREE:

YOU ARE EASY TO UNDERSTAND

YOU ARE LOUD AND CLEAR

YOUR ACTIONS ARE PURE

THERE IS POSITIVE FRUIT ALL AROUND YOU

YOU ARE FLOURISHING

FACT:

FASTING FEELS FRESH

INSPIRATION:

GOD HELPS

Destiny Come Forth

January 3

PRAYER:

MAY YOU PUT ON GOD'S LOVE LIKE A GARMENT

MAY YOU TOUCH EVERYONE YOU MEET

MAY YOU KEEP YOUR EYES WIDE OPEN

MAY YOU REACH OUT TO THOSE IN NEED

MAY YOU BE THERE FOR YOUR FAMILY AND FRIENDS

AMEN

DECREE:

YOU CAN SEE WHAT GOD IS UP TO

YOUR LIFE POINTS IN THE RIGHT DIRECTION

YOU ARE A VERY HOPE FILLED PERSON

YOU ARE SPECIAL TO THE LORD

YOU ARE SPECIAL TO ME

FACT:

FASTING GIVES YOU HOPE

INSPIRATION:

IT'S OKAY TO ASK FOR HELP WHEN YOU NEED IT

Destiny Come Forth

January 4

PRAYER:

MAY YOU FEEL REFRESHED

MAY YOU FEEL READY FOR THE DAY

MAY YOU SHINE BRIGHT WITH THE GOOD NEWS

MAY YOU LOOK FOR DIVINE OPPORTUNITIES

MAY YOU TESTIFY BOLDLY

AMEN

DECREE:

YOU DO SO MUCH

EVERYTHING YOU DO IS GREATLY APPRECIATED

YOU DO NOT NEED THE LIMELIGHT

YOU DO EVERYTHING AS IF YOU ARE DOING IT FOR THE LORD

YOU ARE RELENTLESS

FACT:

FASTING ILLUMINATES YOUR DESTINY

INSPIRATION:

PEACE, HOPE, AND JOY TO YOU

Destiny Come Forth

January 5

PRAYER:

MAY YOU MOVE FORWARD WITH GRACE

MAY YOU STAY ON THE FRONTLINES

MAY YOU LOOK UP TO GOD

MAY YOU LET GO OF THE OLD

MAY YOU REACH TOWARD ALL THAT IS NEW

AMEN

DECREE:

YOUR HARVEST IS RIPE

GOD HAS GIVEN YOU A SICKLE

YOU LOOK FOR THE LOST

YOU ARE A GOOD SHEPHERD

YOU TEND OUR FATHER'S FLOCK

FACT:

FASTING PROPELS YOU FORWARD

INSPIRATION:

BE A GOD HOT SPOT

Destiny Come Forth

January 6

PRAYER:

MAY HEALING SURROUND YOU

MAY PEACE SURROUND YOU

MAY JOY SURROUND YOU

MAY HOPE SURROUND YOU

MAY TRUTH SURROUND YOU

DECREE:

YOU HAVE GREAT OPPORTUNITIES RIGHT IN FRONT OF YOU

YOU STRIVE FOR THE BEST

YOU HAVE CHILDLIKE FAITH

YOU BELIEVE THAT EVERYTHING IS POSSIBLE WITH GOD

YOU ARE AN OVERCOMER

AMEN

FACT:

FASTING MOVES YOU FORWARD

INSPIRATION:

PUTTING GOD FIRST WAS THE BEST THING I EVER DID

Destiny Come Forth

January 7

PRAYER:

MAY YOU LIVE YOUR LIFE HAPPY

MAY YOU REACH OUT TO YOUR CLOSE FRIENDS

MAY YOU PLAN FUN ADVENTURES

MAY YOU LEARN MORE EVERY DAY

MAY YOU STAY CLOSE TO GOD

AMEN

DECREE:

YOU ARE CHOSEN

YOU ARE FAVORED

YOU ARE GOLDEN

YOU ARE A KEY

YOU UNLOCK DESTINY

FACT:

FASTING CONVERTS YOUR FOCUS

INSPIRATION:

SNUGGLE UP TO GOD'S LOVE

Destiny Come Forth

January 8

PRAYER:

MAY YOU THINK LIKE A CHAMPION

MAY YOU LIVE YOUR LIFE WORTHY OF THE SACRIFICE JESUS MADE FOR YOU

MAY YOU LOOK UP

MAY YOU PUT GOD FIRST

MAY YOU RISE TO THE OCCASION

AMEN

DECREE:

YOU ARE VALUABLE

YOU ARE MADE BY GOD

YOU IMAGINE THE BEST

YOU BELIEVE FOR MORE

YOU STAND IN COMPLETE CONFIDENCE

FACT:

FASTING SEARCHES GOD'S HEART

INSPIRATION:

KEEP LOOKING FOR YOUR MIRACLES

Destiny Come Forth

January 9

PRAYER:

MAY YOU FEEL THE EXCITEMENT IN THE AIR

MAY YOU BE ENCOURAGED

MAY YOU ROLL FORWARD WITH THE NEW MOMENTUM

MAY YOU EMBRACE THE CHANGES

MAY YOU BE A POSITIVE INFLUENCE

AMEN

DECREE:

YOU ARE A CHAMPION OF THE FAITH

YOU STAY STRONG

YOU SET THE PACE AS YOU RUN THE RACE

YOU DO NOT FAINT OR GROW WEARY

YOU RISE UP AND LIFT OTHERS UP TOO

FACT:

GOD SEES FASTING

INSPIRATION:

ROLL WITH THE HOLY SPIRIT OF GOD

Destiny Come Forth

January 10

PRAYER:

MAY YOU ENCOUNTER GOD IN A NEW WAY

MAY YOU PRESS INTO YOUR DESTINY

MAY YOU LIVE THE LIFE THAT GOD GAVE TO YOU

MAY YOU STEP FORWARD WITH CONFIDENCE

MAY YOU USHER IN REVIVAL

AMEN

DECREE:

YOU WALK IT OUT

YOU BELIEVE FOR THE IMPOSSIBLE

YOU KEEP MOVING FORWARD

YOU ARE DETERMINED TO WIN

YOU KNOW THAT GOD HOLDS YOUR VICTORY

FACT:

FASTING FACES GOD

INSPIRATION:

GOD CAN DO THE IMPOSSIBLE ANYTIME HE WANTS

January 11

PRAYER:

MAY YOU POSITION YOURSELF TO HEAR FROM GOD

MAY YOU STAY A STUDENT

MAY YOU GROW MORE EVERY YEAR

MAY YOU BE QUIET LONG ENOUGH TO HEAR

MAY YOU LET GOD ORDER YOUR STEPS

AMEN

DECREE:

YOU ARE FILLED WITH THE JOY OF THE LORD

YOU CAN'T HELP BUT FIND THE FUNNY SIDE OF LIFE

YOU ARE AN ENCOURAGER

YOU TAP INTO HEAVEN

YOU BRING GOD TO YOUR TOWN

FACT:

FASTING DEEPENS LOVE

INSPIRATION:

WHEN YOU ARE LOW GOD WILL GLOW

Destiny Come Forth

January 12

PRAYER:

MAY YOU FILL THE AIR WITH HOPE

MAY YOU BLESS THOSE IN FRONT OF YOU

MAY YOU KEEP GOD IN MIND

MAY YOU REFLECT HIS LOVE

MAY YOU DO WHAT YOU CAN DO WITH ZEAL

AMEN

DECREE:

YOU ARE VALIANT

YOU ARE ARMED WITH THE LOVE OF GOD

YOU FORGIVE ALL

YOU ARE A CHAMPION OF THE FAITH

YOU ARE SWEET

FACT:

FASTING PREPARES YOUR FUTURE

INSPIRATION:

GOD HEALS HEARTS SO GIVE HIM YOURS TODAY

January 13

PRAYER:

MAY YOU SEE ALL THAT IS GOOD AROUND YOU

MAY YOU DECREE A THING

MAY YOU BELIEVE IN GOD WITH YOUR WHOLE HEART

MAY YOU TRUST IN GOD BE REVIVED

MAY YOU BOLDLY TAKE YOUR PLACE

AMEN

DECREE:

YOU ARE GOOD

YOU ARE HERE FOR THIS TIME FRAME

THE POWER OF GOD IS RISING UP IN YOU

YOU ARE FULL OF GOOD NEWS

YOU BUBBLE UP

FACT:

FASTING REFRESHES EVERYTHING

INSPIRATION:

BE UPBEAT

Destiny Come Forth

January 14

PRAYER:

MAY YOU STAY IN SYNC WITH GOD

MAY YOU FEEL THE FLOW

MAY YOU GO WITH IT

MAY YOU ENJOY ALL OF IT

MAY YOU BE REFRESHED TODAY

AMEN

DECREE:

YOU ARE PRECIOUS

YOU ARE SOLID

YOU DO TERRIFIC THINGS

YOU ARE KIND HEARTED

YOU FOLLOW IN GOD'S FOOTSTEPS

FACT:

FASTING ACCELERATES HOLY THINGS

INSPIRATION:

YOU HAVE PLENTY OF TIME

Destiny Come Forth

January 15

PRAYER:

MAY YOU POP UP GLORIOUSLY

MAY YOU GROW TALL

MAY YOU BOOM WHERE YOU ARE PLANTED

MAY YOU SERVE WHOLEHEARTEDLY

MAY YOU ALWAYS THRIVE

AMEN

DECREE:

YOU HUSTLE

YOU GET THE JOB DONE

YOU DO WHAT YOU CAN FOR OTHERS

YOU ARE GENEROUS

YOU CAN MULTITASK

FACT:

FASTING FERTILIZES YOUR LIFE

INSPIRATION:

ARMY ARISE

Destiny Come Forth

January 16

PRAYER:

MAY YOU FIND GOD'S TREASURES

MAY YOU SHARE HIS WEALTH

MAY YOU GIVE OUT SALVATION

MAY YOU WALK IN PURITY POWER

MAY YOU STAY REFUELED

AMEN

DECREE:

YOU ARE GOD'S BELOVED CHILD

GOD ADORES YOU

YOU ARE CHERISHED

YOU CAN FEEL THE LOVE

YOUR SELF WORTH IS INCREASING

FACT:

FASTING RELIEVES PAIN

INSPIRATION:

SUBMERGE YOURSELF IN GOD'S LOVE

January 17

PRAYER:

MAY YOU FIND TRUE HAPPINESS

MAY YOU HELP OTHER PEOPLE ENJOY LIFE

MAY YOU SEEK GOD FOR ALL THE ANSWERS

MAY YOU LEARN TO HEAR HIS VOICE

MAY YOU CONTINUE TO GROW WISE

AMEN

DECREE:

YOU ARE PRUDENT

YOU USE GOD'S WISDOM TO HELP PEOPLE

YOU CARE ABOUT THE PEOPLE IN FRONT OF YOU

YOU KNOW HOW MUCH GOD LOVES ALL OF US

YOU ARE DILIGENT

FACT:

FASTING WORKS FAST

INSPIRATION:

SEEK GOD AND GROW

Destiny Come Forth

January 18

PRAYER:

MAY YOU THINK OF WAYS TO BLESS PEOPLE

MAY YOU LOOK OUTWARD

MAY YOU REACH OUT WITH LOVE

MAY YOU MAKE THE NECESSARY CHANGES

MAY YOU PIONEER A NEW MINISTRY OF HELP

AMEN

DECREE:

YOU ARE LOVED BY GOD

GOD HAS MADE YOU BY HAND INTO HIS IMAGE

YOU CAN CONQUER ALL PROBLEMS WITH HIS POWER

GOD BACKS YOU UP

YOU HAVE BEEN SET FREE INDEED

FACT:

FASTING BREAKS FOOD ADDICTION

INSPIRATION:

STAY FOCUSED ON CHANGING YOURSELF

Destiny Come Forth

January 19

PRAYER:

MAY YOU PREPARE THE WAY

MAY YOU TESTIFY LOUDLY

MAY YOU SHARE GOD'S HOPE

MAY YOU BE A BRAVE EXAMPLE

MAY YOU LEAD WITH YOUR LIFESTYLE

AMEN

DECREE:

YOU ARE A NATURAL BORN LEADER

YOU HAVE FOUND YOUR PLACE TO LEAD

YOU TAKE YOUR TIME AND DO THINGS RIGHT

GOD LOVES THE WAY YOU LIVE

YOU HAVE STYLE

FACT:

FASTING CHANGES EVERYTHING

INSPIRATION:

GOD WANTS YOU TO BE HAPPY, PROSPER, AND SUCCEED

Destiny Come Forth

January 20

PRAYER:

MAY YOU ALWAYS REMEMBER WHO YOU ARE

MAY YOU KNOW WHO GOD IS IN YOUR LIFE

MAY YOU STAY HOPE FULL

MAY YOU SEEK THE BEST

MAY YOU TRY HARD EVERY DAY

AMEN

DECREE:

YOU ARE ON YOUR WAY UP THE HOLY MOUNTAIN OF GOD

YOU ARE A GOOD CLIMBER

YOU TAKE TIME TO REST

YOU ARE FILLED WITH EXPECTATION

DEEP DOWN YOU KNOW THE WAY

FACT:

FASTING INITIATES GOD'S POWER IN YOUR LIFE

INSPIRATION:

GOD HAS A WAY

Destiny Come Forth

January 21

PRAYER:

MAY YOU SPEAK WORDS OF LIFE

MAY YOU GET ALONG WITH OTHERS

MAY YOU REFRESH YOURSELF WITH GOD'S WORD

MAY YOU GO OUT AND REFRESH OTHERS

MAY YOU BELIEVE THE GOOD NEWS OF GOD

AMEN

DECREE:

YOU ARE FAITHFUL

YOU REAP JOY

GOOD THINGS COME TO YOU

YOU DO GOOD THINGS

YOU CARE ABOUT OTHERS

FACT:

FASTING REVS YOUR LIFE

INSPIRATION:

COME FORTH AND SPRING UP

Destiny Come Forth

January 22

PRAYER:

MAY YOU LINE UP YOUR DAY WITH THE WORD

MAY YOU JOIN IN WITH THE SAINTS

MAY YOU TAKE TIME TO WORSHIP GOD

MAY YOU REST AND RELAX

MAY YOU EXPERIENCE GREAT PEACE

AMEN

DECREE:

YOU ARE CHOSEN

YOU ARE TRAINED UP

YOU SHARE WHAT YOU KNOW

YOU LOVE TO SEE OTHER PEOPLE GROW

YOU ARE A GOOD PERSON

FACT:

FASTING HELPS YOU GROW

INSPIRATION:

GOD LOVES YOU WITH THE BEST LOVE

Destiny Come Forth

January 23

PRAYER:

MAY YOU LOOK INTO GOD'S EYES

MAY YOU FEEL HIS PEACE

MAY YOU KNOW THAT YOU ARE LOVED

MAY YOUR FAITH BE RENEWED

MAY YOUR GOALS BE IGNITED

AMEN

DECREE:

YOU ARE STRONG AND COURAGEOUS

YOU ARE FILLED WITH GUSTO

YOU SUPERCHARGE THE ATMOSPHERE

YOU HAVE LOTS OF ENERGY

YOU ARE SINCERE

FACT:

FASTING FORTIFIES YOUR DIRECTION

INSPIRATION:

BE AN INSPIRATION

Destiny Come Forth

January 24

PRAYER:

MAY YOU GO FORWARD REFRESHED

MAY YOU WALK AND TALK LIKE A CHAMPION

MAY YOU LOOK AND FEEL LIKE JESUS

MAY YOU TRUST GOD'S DIRECTION

MAY YOU PROCLAIM HIS GOODNESS

AMEN

DECREE:

YOU ARE REVVED UP

YOU ARE READY TO GET SOMEWHERE TODAY

YOU SOUND THE HORN

YOU MAKE WAY

YOU PRESS ON THE ACCELERATOR

FACT:

FASTING FINDS TREASURE

INSPIRATION:

REMEMBER THE VICTORY

Destiny Come Forth

January 25

PRAYER:

MAY YOU FIND WHAT YOU ARE LOOKING FOR

MAY YOU KNOW WHAT IS IMPORTANT

MAY YOU SEEK THE FACE OF GOD

MAY YOU BELIEVE FOR MORE PEACE

MAY YOU HEAR THE TRUTH

AMEN

DECREE:

YOU LOVE SHARING THE GOOD NEWS

YOU GIVE YOUR ALL AND ALL

YOU ARE FUN

YOU ARE FUNNY

YOU SHIFT THE ATMOSPHERE WITH JOY

FACT:

FASTING SETS A FOUNDATION

INSPIRATION:

THROW YOUR NETS OUT AGAIN

Destiny Come Forth

January 26

PRAYER:

MAY YOU TURN UP THE VOLUME

MAY YOU GO ABOUT DOING GOOD

MAY YOU REACH OUT WITH GOD'S LOVE

MAY YOU BELIEVE FOR MIRACLES

MAY YOU PRESS IN AND PRESS ON

AMEN

DECREE:

YOU ARE TUNED IN

YOU ARE TURNED UP

YOU ARE READY TO GO

YOU ARE ALWAYS UP TO SOMETHING GOOD

YOU KEEP GOING

FACT:

FASTING HELPS A LOT

INSPIRATION:

IT'S TIME TO BUILD

Destiny Come Forth

January 27

PRAYER:

MAY YOU FIND REFUGE IN GOD

MAY YOU STAY IN HIS FACE

MAY YOU SHOW OTHER PEOPLE THE WAY TO HAVE PEACE

MAY YOU STAY STRONG

MAY YOU REJOICE IN GOD'S PROTECTION

AMEN

DECREE:

YOU ARE A LIGHT IN THE DARKNESS

YOU GET BRIGHTER AND BRIGHTER

YOU SHINE WITH THE LOVE OF GOD

YOU ARE A BLESSING TO EVERYONE AROUND YOU

YOU STAND TALL

FACT:

FASTING SAVES MONEY

INSPIRATION:

MOTIVATE OTHERS

Destiny Come Forth

January 28

PRAYER:

MAY YOU BREAK THROUGH ON EVERY SIDE

MAY YOU STAY CONFIDENT

MAY YOU USE YOUR SWORD

MAY YOU STAY ARMORED

MAY YOU COME FORTH ABUNDANTLY

AMEN

DECREE:

YOU KNOW WHERE YOUR SATISFACTION COMES FROM

YOU DO WHAT GOD WANTS

YOU LIVE A PEACE FILLED LIFE

YOU ARE SECURE IN YOUR DESTINY

YOU TELL THE TRUTH

FACT:

FASTING CREATES WEALTH

INSPIRATION:

YOU ARE THE BEST

Destiny Come Forth

January 29

PRAYER:

MAY YOU HEAR THE WORD OF GOD

MAY YOU DO THE WORD OF GOD

MAY YOU PREACH THE WORD OF GOD

MAY YOUR LIFE BE A HOLY EPISTLE

MAY YOUR LIFE HIT THE MARK

AMEN

DECREE:

YOU ARE WISE

YOU SHARE YOUR WEALTH OF KNOWLEDGE

YOU CARE ABOUT OTHERS

YOU DO YOUR BEST

YOU GIVE AND GIVE AND GIVE

FACT:

FASTING STACKS UP BLESSINGS

INSPIRATION:

KNOW YOUR ROLE AND ROLL

Destiny Come Forth

January 30

PRAYER:

MAY YOU STEP INTO GOD'S PLANS FOR YOU

MAY YOU HELP OTHER PEOPLE FIND THEIR PLACE TOO

MAY YOU GO FORWARD WITH POWER

MAY YOU BRING HOPE

MAY YOU STAY PEACE FULL

AMEN

DECREE:

YOU ARE WORTH IT

YOUR PRICE IS HIGH

YOU HAVE BEEN SALVAGED

YOU ARE BEING RECYCLED

EVERYTHING WILL BE MADE NEW FOR YOU

FACT:

FASTING FIRMS UP YOUR LIFE

INSPIRATION:

I WOULD RATHER BE DIFFERENT THAN BE THE SAME

Destiny Come Forth

January 31

PRAYER:

MAY YOU FEEL GREAT INSIDE

MAY YOU SEE THE GOODNESS OF GOD SHINE ALL AROUND YOU

MAY YOU BRIGHTEN UP THE FUTURE

MAY YOU POINT TO OUR GREAT POTENTIAL

MAY YOU SHOW EVERYONE WHAT GOD IS DOING

AMEN

DECREE:

TODAY YOU ARE ON TOP OF IT

YOU ARE LIKE A LAMP STAND

YOU BRIGHTEN UP THE ROOM

YOU GET YOUR ENERGY FROM GOD

YOU ILLUMINATE THE POSSIBILITIES

FACT:

FASTING REVIVES EVERYTHING

INSPIRATION:

GOD MADE YOU GREAT

Destiny Come Forth

February 1

PRAYER:

MAY YOUR LIFE LIGHT UP

MAY YOU FIND YOUR PLACE TO PLUG IN

MAY YOU STAY SAFE

MAY YOU ONLY DO WHAT GOD ASKS

MAY YOU THRIVE ALIVE

AMEN

DECREE:

YOU ARE HOLY

YOU ARE FULL OF GOD'S GLORY

YOU WERE CREATED TO DO GREAT EXPLOITS

GOD WATCHES OVER YOU

THE HOLY ANGELS APPLAUD YOU

FACT:

FASTING TURNS ON THE LIGHTS

INSPIRATION:

GOD HAS HIS EYE ON YOU EVEN IN THE EYE OF THE STORM

Destiny Come Forth

February 2

PRAYER:

MAY YOU FIND FAVOR

MAY YOU BUMP INTO MIRACLES

MAY YOU SPREAD THE GOOD NEWS

MAY YOU BIRTH REVIVAL

MAY YOU BRING RESTORATION

AMEN

DECREE:

YOU KEEP YOUR HEAD DOWN WHEN YOU ARE WORKING

YOU FOCUS ON THE TASK AT HAND

YOU ARE A FINISHER

YOU SUCCEED

YOU ACCOMPLISH MANY GREAT THINGS

FACT:

FASTING FUELS YOUR ENGINE

INSPIRATION:

BREATHE IN GOD'S GOODNESS

February 3

PRAYER:

MAY YOU FIND STRENGTH

MAY YOU BE ENCOURAGED

MAY YOU BELIEVE FOR BREAKTHROUGH

MAY YOU PUSH INTO GOD

MAY YOU FOCUS ON THE GOOD NEWS

AMEN

DECREE:

YOU ARE GLOWING

YOU ARE FULL OF GOOD NEWS

YOU ARE BURSTING WITH JOY

YOU HAVE BEEN REFRESHED

YOU ARE READY FOR THIS DAY

FACT:

FASTING STRENGTHENS YOU

INSPIRATION:

WORK ON SOMETHING

Destiny Come Forth

February 4

PRAYER:

MAY YOU KEEP YOUR HEAD HIGH

MAY YOU REACH TO GOD

MAY YOU LET GOD LEAD

MAY YOU FOLLOW GOD EVER SO CLOSELY

MAY YOU KEEP UP

AMEN

DECREE:

GOD TALKS TO YOU

YOU SHARE WHAT GOD SAYS

YOU HONOR GOD

YOU RESPECT OTHER PEOPLE

YOU ARE A GENUINE SERVANT

FACT:

FASTING FINDS LOVE

INSPIRATION:

BUILD YOUR FAITH

Destiny Come Forth

February 5

PRAYER:

MAY YOU WALK RIGHT

MAY YOU STAND TALL

MAY YOU SPEAK BLESSINGS

MAY YOU HELP YOUR NEIGHBOR

MAY YOU STAY STRONG

AMEN

DECREE:

YOU ARE FULL OF HOPE

YOU ENCOURAGE EVERYONE YOU MEET

YOU ARE SUCH A GOOD EXAMPLE

YOU LEAVE A BRIGHT TRAIL TO FOLLOW

YOU ARE ABLAZE

FACT:

FASTING IS A SACRIFICE

INSPIRATION:

KEEP GETTING BETTER

February 6

PRAYER:

MAY YOU SEE THE SILVER LINING

MAY YOU COME UP AS PURE GOLD

MAY THE WISDOM OF GOD SURROUND YOU

MAY YOU LIVE IN THE RIGHT TIME

MAY YOU ECHO HEAVEN

AMEN

DECREE:

YOU KEEP MOVING FORWARD

YOU MAKE THE MOST OUT OF EVERY MOMENT

YOU ARE FUNSHINE

YOU GLOW WITH GOD'S GOODNESS

YOU BEAM HIGH

FACT:

FASTING IMPROVES CIRCULATION

INSPIRATION:

DO THE RIGHT THINGS

Destiny Come Forth

February 7

PRAYER:

MAY YOU HEAR THE LORD TODAY

MAY YOU BE ENCOURAGED

MAY YOU FIGHT FOR WHAT IS RIGHT

MAY YOU HELP YOUR NEIGHBOR

MAY YOU BE A GOOD EXAMPLE

AMEN

DECREE:

YOU ARE STRONG-HEADED

YOUR FAITH PUSHES YOU

YOU HEAR THE TRUTH

YOU DO THE RIGHT THINGS

YOU ARE ALL IN

FACT:

FASTING STARTS YOUR DAY OFF RIGHT

INSPIRATION:

SHOUT FOR JOY

Destiny Come Forth

February 8

PRAYER:

MAY YOU WALK THE WALK

MAY YOU SHOW THE LOVE OF GOD

MAY YOU BE MERCY FULL

MAY YOU GIVE GOD YOUR BEST

MAY YOU BE SURROUNDED BY FAVOR

AMEN

DECREE:

YOU ARE A LIGHT

YOU ARE FULL OF GREAT IDEAS

YOU BRING THE NOT SO OBVIOUS TO THE FOREFRONT

YOU OPEN DOORS

YOU PAID THE PRICE

FACT:

FASTING IS UPLIFTING

INSPIRATION:

LEAVE A LEGACY OF FORGIVENESS

Destiny Come Forth

February 9

PRAYER:

MAY YOU RUN THE RACE TO WIN

MAY YOU FIGHT THE GOOD FIGHT

MAY THE STRENGTH OF GOD BE IN YOU

MAY YOU FIND FAVOR

MAY YOU SHARE THE VICTORY

AMEN

DECREE:

YOU ARE COURAGEOUS

YOU FEAR NOTHING

YOU TRUST IN GOD'S JUSTICE

YOU WAIT PATIENTLY

YOU LIVE ON THE OTHER SIDE OF THE FINISH LINE

FACT:

FASTING REVEALS THE PLAN OF GOD

INSPIRATION:

FOLLOW IN JESUS' FOOTSTEPS

Destiny Come Forth

February 10

PRAYER:

MAY YOU FIND YOUR WAY

MAY YOU BOLDLY WALK WITH GOD

MAY YOU SEEK THE TRUTH

MAY YOU USE YOUR FAITH

MAY YOU LIVE A LIFE OF JOY

AMEN

DECREE:

YOU ARE A RAY OF SUNSHINE

YOUR SMILE WARMS HEARTS

YOU ARE SINCERE

YOU ARE KIND

YOU ARE THE BEST YOU

FACT:

FASTING REFRESHES EVERYTHING

INSPIRATION:

FEAR NOT

Destiny Come Forth

February 11

PRAYER:

MAY YOU LIVE LONG

MAY YOU BE FULL OF JOY

MAY YOU BE FULL OF HOPE

MAY YOU RECEIVE FAVOR FROM GOD

MAY YOU SHARE HIS LOVE

AMEN

DECREE:

THE JOY OF THE LORD CONSUMES YOU

YOU ARE FULL OF COMPASSION

YOU WALK THE TALK

YOU ARE GENUINE

YOU ARE AUTHENTIC

FACT:

FASTING DUSTS OFF VISION

INSPIRATION:

LIVE ALIVE

Destiny Come Forth

February 12

PRAYER:

MAY YOU REST IN GOD

MAY YOU ENJOY BEING HELD BY HIM

MAY GOD'S PEACE CONSUME YOU

MAY YOU BECOME A REFUGE OF LOVE

MAY YOU SHELTER MANY

AMEN

DECREE:

YOU ARE READY

YOU ARE WELL TRAINED

YOU ARE A HOLY ATHLETE

YOU ARE SKILLED

YOU ARE GIFTED

FACT:

FASTING LINES THINGS UP

INSPIRATION:

FIND FRIENDS WHO HAVE FOUND GOD

Destiny Come Forth

February 13

PRAYER:

MAY YOU SEEK GOD FIRST

MAY YOU DISCOVER YOUR PURPOSE

MAY YOU SIMPLY OBEY GOD

MAY YOU GO WHERE GOD SENDS YOU

MAY YOU DO WHAT GOD WANTS YOU TO DO

AMEN

DECREE:

YOU ARE THE JOY OF THE LORD

GOD'S LOVE SHINES ALL OVER YOUR FACE

YOU ARE GOOD INSIDE AND OUT

THE GOOD NEWS HAS SET YOU FREE

YOU SET OTHER PEOPLE FREE

FACT:

FASTING PUSHES THINGS AROUND

INSPIRATION:

LOVE HARD

Destiny Come Forth

February 14

PRAYER:

MAY YOU ENJOY GOD'S TRUE LOVE

MAY YOU SEEK THE ONE TRUE GOD

MAY YOU SHARE THE LOVE OF GOD TODAY WITH OTHERS

MAY YOU BE VALIANT

MAY YOU ALWAYS BELIEVE FOR THE BEST

AMEN

DECREE:

YOU ARE EXTRAVAGANT

YOU ARE FLAMBOYANT

YOU ARE EXTRAORDINARY

YOU ARE FULL OF ENERGY

YOU NEVER AGE

FACT:

FASTING OPENS YOUR EYES

INSPIRATION:

IT'S WORTH IT TO EARTH IT

YOU CAN BRING HEAVEN TO EARTH

Destiny Come Forth

February 15

PRAYER:

MAY YOU FEEL CONFIDENT

MAY YOU STAND UP STRONG

MAY YOU KNOW THAT GOD LOVES YOU

MAY YOU HAVE EYES TO SEE YOUR BLESSINGS

MAY YOUR EARS HEAR THE VOICE OF GOD

AMEN

DECREE:

YOU EXPECT THE BEST

YOU DESERVE THE BEST

YOU BRING THE BEST

THE BEST IS YET TO COME

YOU ARE THE BEST PERSON THAT YOU CAN BE

FACT:

FASTING MAKES SENSE

INSPIRATION:

GOD IS WITH YOU

Destiny Come Forth

February 16

PRAYER:

MAY YOU FOLLOW GOD'S DESIGN

MAY YOU ENJOY THE PROCESS

MAY YOU HEAR THE HEART OF GOD

MAY YOU MARCH TO THE BEAT

MAY YOU LEAP FOR JOY TODAY

AMEN

DECREE:

YOU ARE HOLY TO THE LORD

YOU ARE CHOSEN

YOU ARE PRICELESS

YOU ARE VALUED

YOU ARE IRREPLACEABLE

FACT:

FASTING SAVES ENERGY

INSPIRATION:

FOLLOW GOD INTENTLY

Destiny Come Forth

February 17

PRAYER:

MAY YOU BREAK FREE FROM MONOTONY

MAY YOU RUN FOR GOD

MAY YOU EMBRACE A NEW ADVENTURE

MAY YOU BELIEVE IN THE IMPOSSIBLE

MAY YOU STRIKE WHEN THE IRON IS HOT

AMEN

DECREE:

YOU ARE PROTECTED BY GOD

GOD LOVES YOU

YOU ARE PART OF GOD'S FAMILY

YOU ARE GOD'S PROPERTY

YOU ARE FERTILE SOIL

FACT:

FASTING CARRIES YOU FORWARD

INSPIRATION:

RISE UP

Destiny Come Forth

February 18

PRAYER:

MAY YOU MAKE QUALITY DECISIONS

MAY YOU LOOK TO GOD'S WORD

MAY YOU STAY IN LINE

MAY YOU GAIN GROUND

MAY YOU MAKE A MARK

AMEN

DECREE:

YOU LOVE TO HANG AROUND JESUS

YOU ARE CLOSE FRIENDS WITH THE LORD

YOU LEARN MORE EVERY DAY

YOU SEEK THE TRUTH

YOU FOLLOW AFTER GOD

FACT:

FASTING BRINGS OUT YOUR BEST

INSPIRATION:

TAKE A STAND

Destiny Come Forth

February 19

PRAYER:

MAY YOU STAY PEACE FULL

MAY YOU TRUST GOD WITH EVERYTHING

MAY YOU BELIEVE THE WORD OF GOD

MAY YOU ARM YOURSELF WITH GOD'S POWER

MAY YOU LEARN THE WARFARE SKILLS

AMEN

DECREE:

YOU ARE SINCERE

YOU ARE TOP QUALITY

YOU ARE RIGHT ON TRACK

YOU KNOW YOUR PURPOSE

YOU HEAR FROM GOD

FACT:

FASTING REIGNITES DIRECTION

INSPIRATION:

BE FULL OF CHRIST

Destiny Come Forth

February 20

PRAYER:

MAY YOU FIND PEACE

MAY YOU FIND JOY

MAY YOU FIND HOPE

MAY YOU FIND LOVE

MAY YOU FIND GOD

AMEN

DECREE:

YOU ARE COMPASSIONATE

YOUR EYES ARE WIDE OPEN

YOU CAN SEE WHO NEEDS YOUR HELP

YOU ARE A SERVANT OF THE LORD

YOU DO EVERYTHING AS IS YOU ARE DOING IT FOR HIM

FACT:

FASTING IGNITES ZEAL

INSPIRATION:

GOD IS EXTREMELY FLEXIBLE YET EXPLICIT AT THE SAME TIME

Destiny Come Forth

February 21

PRAYER:

MAY YOU FIND YOUR BALANCE

MAY YOU ENJOY YOUR WORK

MAY YOU ENJOY YOUR REST

MAY YOU ENJOY THE SEASONS AS THEY CHANGE

MAY YOU ENJOY ALL YOUR DAYS

AMEN

DECREE:

YOU ARE STRONG IN THE LORD

YOU STRENGTHEN OTHERS

YOU PUT YOUR BEST FOOT FORWARD

YOU ENJOY ADVENTURE

GOD LEADS YOU

FACT:

FASTING SETS YOU FREE

INSPIRATION:

LOVE TRULY IS THE GREATEST

Destiny Come Forth

February 22

PRAYER:

MAY YOU LIVE THE LIFE YOU LOVE

MAY YOU SHARE THE LOVE WITH OTHERS

MAY LOVE ALWAYS BE YOUR AIM

MAY YOU SHOOT HIGH

MAY YOU THRIVE

AMEN

DECREE:

YOU ARE FULL OF GRACE

YOU SEEK GOD'S FACE

YOU HEAR GOD'S VOICE

YOU SPEND QUALITY TIME WITH GOD

YOU ARE CENTERED

FACT:

FASTING PREPARES YOUR HEART

INSPIRATION:

GOD MOTIVATES

Destiny Come Forth

February 23

PRAYER:

MAY YOU ENJOY THE SEASONS

MAY YOU LOOK TO LOVE OTHERS

MAY YOU DO SOMETHING SPECIAL

MAY YOU GO THE EXTRA MILE

MAY YOU TAKE TIME TO SAVOR

AMEN

DECREE:

YOU ARE CHOSEN

YOU ARE SET APART

YOU ARE GODS

YOU ARE VALUABLE

YOU ARE LOVED

FACT:

FASTING GOES THE DISTANCE

INSPIRATION:

PUT IN EFFORT

Destiny Come Forth

February 24

PRAYER:

MAY YOU RUN INTO THIS DAY FULL OF JOY

MAY YOU PULL ON GOD

MAY YOU BRING GOD CLOSER

MAY YOU HEAR FROM HEAVEN

MAY YOU RELEASE COMPASSION ON THE EARTH

AMEN

DECREE:

JESUS CHRIST IS YOUR ROLE MODEL

YOU GO AND DO THE SAME

YOU PRAISE GOD ALL DAY LONG

YOU DO GOOD TO ALL

YOU BELIEVE THE TRUTH

FACT:

FASTING SETS THINGS STRAIGHT

INSPIRATION:

POINT OUT POTENTIAL

Destiny Come Forth

February 25

PRAYER:

MAY YOU LOVE WHAT YOU DO

MAY YOU DO WHAT YOU LOVE

MAY GOD GIVE YOU PEACE

MAY YOU ENJOY JOY

MAY YOUR HOPE COMPEL YOU

AMEN

DECREE:

YOU ARE HAPPY

YOU ARE SECURE

YOU ARE SAFE

YOU ARE BLESSED

YOU ARE FULL OF GOD

FACT:

FASTING FINDS ENERGY

INSPIRATION:

USE YOUR GOD GIVEN GIFTS AND TALENTS

Destiny Come Forth

February 26

PRAYER:

MAY YOU TASTE AND SEE THE GOODNESS OF THE LORD

MAY YOU SHARE IN HIS LOVE

MAY YOU FEED THE HUNGRY IN YOUR TOWN

MAY WHAT GOD CARES ABOUT CARRY YOU

MAY GOD INTERVENE SUPERNATURALLY

AMEN

DECREE:

YOU WILL GAIN STRENGTH

YOU WILL CARRY MANY TO THE FINISH LINE

YOU WILL PUSH THROUGH

YOU WILL TOW THE LINE

YOU WILL REVIVE ALL

FACT:

FASTING TAKES IN HOLY NUTRITION

INSPIRATION:

DIVE INTO THE LOVE OF GOD TODAY

Destiny Come Forth

February 27

PRAYER:

MAY YOU REACH OUT OF YOUR COMFORT ZONE

MAY YOU SHARE WHAT YOU HAVE

MAY YOU KEEP GOING

MAY YOU KEEP GIVING

MAY YOU LIVE IN THE TRUTH

AMEN

DECREE:

YOU ARE AN ORIGINAL

GOD CREATED YOU WITH A SPECIFIC PURPOSE

ONLY YOU CAN DO WHAT GOD HAS DESIGNED YOU TO DO

AS YOU SHARE YOUR GIFTS IT HELPS US ALL

YOU ARE SAVED

FACT:

FASTING IS AN ART

INSPIRATION:

STOP LOOK AND LISTEN TO GOD

Destiny Come Forth

February 28

PRAYER:

MAY YOUR FAITH INCREASE

MAY YOU STAND UP FOR GOD

MAY YOU KNOW THE TRUTH

MAY YOU BE BRAVE

MAY YOU ENCOURAGE MANY TODAY

AMEN

DECREE:

GOD HAS EQUIPPED YOU FOR SUCH TIME AS THIS

YOU HAVE BEEN WELL TRAINED

GO IS ALWAYS WITH YOU

YOU ARE A WARRIOR

YOU FIGHT THE GOOD FIGHT WITH FAITH

FACT:

FASTING WITH STRENGTHEN YOU

INSPIRATION:

TRUST GOD

Destiny Come Forth

February 29

PRAYER:

MAY YOU BE A GOOD STEWARD

MAY YOU GIVE MORE THAN YOU TAKE

MAY YOU ENJOY THIS LIFE

MAY YOU MAKE THE MOST OUT OF LIFE

MAY YOU TRUST GOD TO BLESS YOU

AMEN

DECREE:

YOU ARE LIKE A HAPPY HERO

YOU ALWAYS POINT TO THE POSITIVE

YOU ARE FULL OF HOPE

YOU ARE FUNSHINE

YOU ARE A BLESSING

FACT:

FASTING GIVES YOU GREAT TIMING

INSPIRATION:

SOMETIMES IT TAKES A MINUTE TO FIND YOUR NICHE

Destiny Come Forth

March 1

PRAYER:

MAY YOU HAVE A GREAT DAY

MAY YOU SEIZE EVERY OPPORTUNITY

MAY YOU LINE UP WITH GOD

MAY YOU BELIEVE FOR THE BEST

MAY YOU ENCOURAGE SOMEONE ELSE

AMEN

DECREE:

YOU ARE SHARP

YOU ARE A HOLY EDGE

YOU CUT RIGHT THROUGH THE CHAOS

YOU STAY FOCUSED ON GOD

YOU WRITE OUT THE PLANS

FACT:

FASTING IS FOR YOU

INSPIRATION:

BREAKTHROUGH COMES WHEN EVERYTHING ELSE LINES UP

Destiny Come Forth

March 2

PRAYER:

MAY THE JOY OF GOD LEAD YOU

MAY YOU HEAR GOD SPEAK

MAY GOOD NEWS SURROUND YOU

MAY YOU REJOICE OUT LOUD

MAY YOU KNOW GOD IS WITH YOU

AMEN

DECREE:

YOU ARE ON TOP

YOU GO FOR IT

GOD IS IGNITING YOUR VISION

YOU CAN SEE CLEARLY NOW

YOU RUN FOR THE GOAL

FACT:

FASTING SETS YOUR HEART ABLAZE

INSPIRATION:

BE COMPASSION

Destiny Come Forth

March 3

PRAYER:

MAY YOU TRUST GOD

MAY GOD THRUST YOU FORWARD

MAY YOUR FAITH CATAPULT YOU TODAY

MAY YOU TAKE THE LAND

MAY YOU MAKE A JOYFUL STAND

AMEN

DECREE:

YOU LOVE TO HEAR GOD SPEAK

YOU RECOGNIZE HIS VOICE EVERYWHERE

THE HOLY SPIRIT KEEPS YOU ALERT

YOU AWAKEN OTHER PEOPLE

YOU BECOME MORE LIKE JESUS EVERY DAY

FACT:

FASTING UNITES

INSPIRATION:

STAY POSITIVE

Destiny Come Forth

March 4

PRAYER:

MAY YOU FOLLOW GOD WHOLEHEARTEDLY

MAY YOU BE FIRM IN YOUR ADHERENCE

MAY YOU STICK TO GOD'S PLANS

MAY YOU WRITE THEM OUT AND MAKE IT CLEAR

MAY YOU RUN WITH FORERUNNERS

AMEN

DECREE:

YOU ARE A REAL GO GETTER

YOU RUN FOR GOD

GOD BLESSES YOU

YOU BLESS OTHERS

YOUR LIFE IS EXCITING

FACT:

FASTING IS NECESSARY

INSPIRATION:

HIT THE GROUND RUNNING

Destiny Come Forth

March 5

PRAYER:

MAY YOU FOLLOW GOD

MAY YOU DO WHAT HE SAYS

MAY YOU RECRUIT FAMILY

MAY YOU RECRUIT FRIENDS

MAY YOU BE SURROUNDED BY LOVE

AMEN

DECREE:

YOU ARE FRIENDLY

PEOPLE CAN SEE THERE IS SOMETHING DIFFERENT ABOUT YOU

YOU GLOW

YOU FLOW

YOU KNOW HOW MUCH GOD LOVES YOU

FACT:

FASTING GAINS MOMENTUM

INSPIRATION:

WALK IN TOTAL FORGIVENESS

Destiny Come Forth

March 6

PRAYER:

MAY YOU FIND ALL THE RIGHT PLACES

MAY YOU FIND ALL THE RIGHT PEOPLE

MAY YOU BE SUBMITTED BY LOVE

MAY YOU SEEK PEACE

MAY YOU FIND JOY TODAY

AMEN

DECREE:

YOU ARE A TRUE JOY

YOU ARE SO FUN TO BE AROUND

YOU MAKE A BIG DIFFERENCE

YOU ARE IMPORTANT

YOU KEEP THE FAITH

FACT:

FASTING IS NOT EASY BUT SO WORTH IT

INSPIRATION:

GOD IS CREATIVE SO TAP IN

Destiny Come Forth

March 7

PRAYER:

MAY YOU BE SENSITIVE TO GOD

MAY YOU GO WITH HIM

MAY YOU OBEY GOD

MAY YOU DO EVERYTHING HE ASKS

MAY YOU OBEY QUICKLY

AMEN

DECREE:

YOU ARE HOLY

YOU ARE FILLED WITH GOD'S LOVE

YOU SHINE BRIGHT

YOU MAKE A WAY

YOU ARE A GREAT LEADER WHEN YOU FOLLOW GOD

FACT:

FASTING TAKES IT UP A NOTCH

INSPIRATION:

LET GOD REFINE YOU

Destiny Come Forth

March 8

PRAYER:

MAY YOU STAY OPEN TO GOD

MAY YOUR HEART STAY SOFT

MAY YOU OBEY GOD EXPLICITLY

MAY YOU STAND STRONG

MAY YOU PRAY ACCORDING TO GOD'S WILL

AMEN

DECREE:

YOU ARE FASCINATING

GOD IS BLESSING YOUR LIFE

YOU ARE FUN TO WATCH

PEOPLE LEARN A LOT FROM YOU

YOU ARE A PATH

FACT:

FASTING CHANGES THINGS

INSPIRATION:

YOU DON'T HAVE TO MUSTER UP GOD HE IS ALWAYS READY

Destiny Come Forth

March 9

PRAYER:

MAY YOU FACE THIS WEEK WITH FAITH

MAY YOU GET STRONGER AND STRONGER

MAY YOU GAIN MOMENTUM

MAY YOU CREATE A NEW PATH

MAY YOU STAKE YOUR CLAIM

AMEN

DECREE:

YOU KEEP IT FRESH

YOU SEEK GOD EVERYDAY

YOU PLEASE GOD

YOU REACH FOR HIS PROMISES

YOU BLESS EVERYONE

FACT:

FASTING FUELS FAITH

INSPIRATION:

GOD CREATED EVERYTHING OUT OF NOTHING

Destiny Come Forth

March 10

PRAYER:

MAY YOU UNDERSTAND THE DEPTH OF GOD'S LOVE

MAY YOU SHARE THIS TRUTH

MAY YOU GET FIRED UP

MAY YOU ILLUMINATE YOUR AREA FOR GOD

MAY YOU GLOW FORWARD

AMEN

DECREE:

YOU ARE AMAZING

GOD LOVES YOU SO MUCH

YOU GO FORWARD WITH GREAT POWER

YOU AREN'T AFRAID OF ANYTHING

GOD IS WITH YOU

FACT:

FASTING IS A FORCE

INSPIRATION:

PIONEER A NEW PATH

Destiny Come Forth

March 11

PRAYER:

MAY YOU ENJOY YOUR REWARD

MAY YOU BELIEVE FOR MORE

MAY YOU HELP OTHERS BELIEVE

MAY YOU PRESS IN TO GOD

MAY YOU ENJOY HIS SAFETY

AMEN

DECREE:

YOU ARE CHERISHED

YOU ARE SPECIAL

YOU ARE NEEDED

YOU ARE HOLY

YOU ARE WONDERFUL

FACT:

FASTING IS A GREAT HABIT

INSPIRATION:

LOVE IS YOUR GREATEST ASSET

Destiny Come Forth

March 12

PRAYER:

MAY YOU FIND YOUR POSITION

MAY YOU FULFILL YOUR DESTINY

MAY YOU HEAR FROM GOD EVEN MORE CLEARLY

MAY YOU RUN YOUR RACE

MAY YOU STAY AGILE

AMEN

DECREE:

YOU ARE HUMBLE

YOU TURN EVERYTHING OVER TO GOD

YOU TRUST GOD COMPLETELY

YOU FIND REVELATION

YOU SHARE HOPE

FACT:

FASTING HELPS YOU PERSEVERE

INSPIRATION:

JOY AND HOPE IS YOURS

Destiny Come Forth

March 13

PRAYER:

MAY YOU FIGHT THE RIGHT WAR

MAY YOU FIGHT WITH GOD'S POWER

MAY YOU STAY COMPLETE

MAY YOU HEAR THE TRUTH

MAY YOU SET PEOPLE FREE

AMEN

DECREE:

GOD IS SPECIFIC WITH YOU

YOU OBEY GOD

YOU ARE ALERT

YOU PAY ATTENTION TO GOD

YOU SEE THE SIGNS ALL AROUND YOU

FACT:

FASTING FIRES YOU UP

INSPIRATION:

REACH OUT TO THE LOST AND LONELY

Destiny Come Forth

March 14

PRAYER:

MAY YOU STAND STRONG

MAY YOU BE FILLED WITH GOD'S POWER

MAY YOU OBEY GOD SWIFTLY

MAY YOU ONLY GO WHERE HE SENDS YOU

MAY YOU BE BRAVE

AMEN

DECREE:

YOU ARE MORE THAN A CONQUEROR

YOU ARE STRONG

YOU ARE CHOSEN BY GOD TO ACCELERATE

YOU ARE READY FOR WHAT IS NEXT

YOU ARE SWIFT

FACT:

FASTING TWIRLS THINGS AROUND

INSPIRATION:

YOU CAN BE A MENTOR

Destiny Come Forth

March 15

PRAYER:

MAY YOU FIND PEACE

MAY YOU TRUST GOD

MAY YOU SHINE HIS LIGHT

MAY YOU MAKE THE WORLD BETTER

MAY YOU REJOICE IN THIS DAY

AMEN

DECREE:

YOU ARE HAPPY

YOU ARE SATISFIED

YOU ARE COMPLETE

YOU ARE A JOY

YOU ARE HEALED

FACT:

FASTING IS SAFE

INSPIRATION:

TRUST YOUR HOLY SENSES

Destiny Come Forth

March 16

PRAYER:

MAY YOU ENJOY EVERY DAY

MAY YOU FEEL MOTIVATED

MAY YOU BE ENCOURAGED

MAY YOU SET THINGS IN ORDER

MAY YOU RISE NOT FALL

AMEN

DECREE:

YOU ARE A SPARK OF ZEAL

YOU ARE A HOLY SURGE ENGINE

YOU BRING REFRESHING HOPE EVERYWHERE YOU GO

YOU ARE GOD'S SERVANT

YOU LOVE PEOPLE

FACT:

FASTING SETS THINGS ON FIRE

INSPIRATION:

FEED YOUR FLOCK

Destiny Come Forth

March 17

PRAYER:

MAY YOU BLAZE A NEW TRAIL

MAY YOUR FOOTPRINTS MARK A PATH OF EXCELLENCE

MAY YOU BLESS THE NEXT GENERATION

MAY YOUR LEGACY BE LONG

MAY YOUR BREAKTHROUGH BE EVERLASTING

DECREE:

THE LOVE OF GOD SURROUNDS YOU

YOU ARE A VESSEL OF LOVE

GOD IS "OUR" LOVING FATHER

WE ARE A FAMILY

LET'S ALL LOVE EACH OTHER WELL

FACT:

FASTING LEADS TO VICTORY

INSPIRATION:

LOVE GOD WITH ALL

Destiny Come Forth

March 18

PRAYER:

MAY YOU FEEL ENCOURAGED

MAY NOTHING STOP YOUR PEACE

MAY YOU GIVE AND GIVE AND GIVE

MAY GOD KEEP YOU REFRESHED

MAY YOU REFRESH OTHERS

AMEN

DECREE:

YOU ARE BLESSED

YOU ARE SUGAR COATED

NO MELT DOWNS FOR YOU

YOU ARE SECURE

YOU ARE FOR SURE

FACT:

FASTING CLEANSES

INSPIRATION:

FIND BALANCE

Destiny Come Forth

March 19

PRAYER:

MAY YOU BE FULL FLEDGED

MAY YOU BE WHAT GOD CALLED YOU TO BE

MAY YOU BE IN THE RIGHT PLACE

MAY YOU DO THE RIGHT THING

MAY YOU HEED THE TRUTH

AMEN

DECREE:

YOU ARE A SOLDIER

YOU HAVE BEEN TRAINED BY GOD

YOU HAVE HOLY WEAPONS

YOU KNOW HOW TO USE THEM

YOU ARE SKILLED AT BATTLE

FACT:

FASTING STRETCHES YOUR FAITH

INSPIRATION:

RECOGNIZE THE CLOSED DOORS

Destiny Come Forth

March 20

PRAYER:

MAY YOU LIVE A FREE LIFE

MAY YOU HELP OTHER PEOPLE GET FREE

MAY YOU STAY FREE FROM WORRY

MAY YOU LET GOD FREE UP YOUR TIME

MAY YOU ONLY DO WHAT GOD WANTS YOU TO DO

AMEN

DECREE:

YOU ARE LOVED BY YOUR FAMILY AND FRIENDS

YOU ARE RESPECTED BY YOUR PEERS

YOU ARE IMPORTANT TO YOUR COMMUNITY

YOU LOVE YOUR COUNTRY

YOU BRING VICTORY

FACT:

FASTING STRENGTHENS YOUR FAITH

INSPIRATION:

JOIN A TEAM AND PARTNER UP

Destiny Come Forth

March 21

PRAYER:

MAY YOU ENCOUNTER GOD'S LOVE TODAY

MAY YOU WRESTLE WITH VICTORY UNTIL YOU WIN

MAY YOU HELP OTHER PEOPLE WIN

MAY YOU STAY TRUE TO GOD

MAY YOU STAY TRUE TO YOUR CALL

AMEN

DECREE:

YOU ARE BURSTING FORTH

YOU ARE LIGHTING UP A NEW PATH

YOU ARE READY

YOU ARE A GREAT SOURCE OF ENCOURAGEMENT

YOU ARE LIKE A HOLY STAMPEDE

FACT:

FASTING LEADS THE WAY

INSPIRATION:

DON'T BE AFRAID TO JUMP

Destiny Come Forth

March 22

PRAYER:

MAY YOU FOLLOW GOD TODAY

MAY YOU STAY NICE AND CLOSE TO HIM

MAY YOU BLAZE A NEW TRAIL

MAY YOU PIONEER A NEW PATH FOR OTHERS

MAY YOU TRUST GOD WITH EVERYTHING

AMEN

DECREE:

YOU ARE WELL RESPECTED

GOD SEES YOU

YOU ARE OPEN TO NEW OPPORTUNITIES

YOU DO YOUR PART

GOD PROTECTS YOU

FACT:

FASTING BRINGS PEACE

INSPIRATION:

GOD MAKES IT EASY

Destiny Come Forth

March 23

PRAYER:

MAY YOU ENJOY YOUR LIFE

MAY YOU ALWAYS LOOK TO GOD

MAY YOU STAY POSITIVE

MAY YOU REJOICE WITH OTHERS

MAY YOU DO SOMETHING CHRISTLIKE

AMEN

DECREE:

YOU ARE TOP NOTCH

YOU KEEP ON GIVING

YOU REACH UP TO GOD FOR STRENGTH

YOU ARE SUPERSIZED

YOU ARE HOLY GROUND

FACT:

FASTING FIGHTS OFF NORMAL

INSPIRATION:

CHANGE ISN'T EASY BUT BREAK THE CHAINS ANYWAYS

Destiny Come Forth

March 24

PRAYER:

MAY YOU RUN INTO YOUR DAY FULL OF JOY

MAY YOU PULL ON GOD

MAY YOU BRING GOD CLOSER

MAY YOU HEAR FROM HEAVEN

MAY YOU RELEASE COMPASSION ON EARTH

AMEN

DECREE:

YOU ARE EXTRAVAGANT

YOU ARE FLAMBOYANT

YOU ARE EXTRAORDINARY

YOU ARE FULL OF ENERGY

YOU NEVER AGE

FACT:

FASTING BRINGS REVIVAL

INSPIRATION:

RECOGNIZE THE OPEN DOORS

Destiny Come Forth

March 25

PRAYER:

MAY YOU WALK THE TALK

MAY YOU SHOW THE LOVE OF GOD

MAY YOU BE MERCY FULL

MAY YOU GIVE YOUR BEST

MAY YOU BE SURROUNDED BY FAVOR

AMEN

DECREE:

YOU ARE A LIGHT

YOU ARE FULL OF GREAT IDEAS

YOU BRING THE NOT SO OBVIOUS TO THE FOREFRONT

YOU OPEN DOORS

YOU PAID THE PRICE

FACT:

FASTING IS UPLIFTING

INSPIRATION:

YOU ARE CHOSEN

Destiny Come Forth

March 26

PRAYER:

MAY YOU RUN THE RACE TO WIN

MAY YOU FIGHT THE GOOD FIGHT

MAY THE STRENGTH OF GOD BE IN YOU

MAY YOU FIND FAVOR

MAY YOU SHARE THE VICTORY

AMEN

DECREE:

YOU ARE COURAGEOUS

YOU FEAR NOTHING

YOU TRUST IN GOD'S JUSTICE

YOU WAIT PATIENTLY

YOU LIVE ON THE OTHER SIDE OF THE FINISH LINE

FACT:

FASTING REVEALS THE PLAN OF GOD

INSPIRATION:

STAY REFRESHED

Destiny Come Forth

March 27

PRAYER:

MAY YOU FIND YOUR WAY

MAY YOU BOLDLY WALK WITH GOD

MAY YOU SEEK THE TRUTH

MAY YOU USE YOUR FAITH

MAY YOU LIVE A LIFE OF JOY

AMEN

DECREE:

YOU ARE A RAY OF SUNSHINE

YOUR SMILE WARMS HEARTS

YOU ARE SINCERE

YOU ARE KIND

YOU ARE THE BEST

FACT:

FASTING REVEALS YOUR TEAM

INSPIRATION:

YOUR TIME IS VALUABLE

Destiny Come Forth

March 28

PRAYER:

MAY YOU LIVE LONG

MAY YOU BE FULL OF JOY

MAY YOU BE FULL OF HOPE

MAY YOU RECEIVE FAVOR FROM GOD

MAY YOU SHARE HIS LOVE

AMEN

DECREE:

YOU ARE BOLD

YOU ARE SOLID

YOUR FAITH IS SECURE

YOUR HEART IS HAPPY

YOU ARE FILLED WITH HOPE

FACT:

FASTING RESTORES HOPE

INSPIRATION:

ASSUME THE BEST

Destiny Come Forth

March 29

PRAYER:

MAY YOU REST IN GOD

MAY YOU ENJOY BEING HELD BY HIM

MAY GOD'S PEACE CONSUME YOU

MAY YOU BECOME A REFUGE OF LOVE

MAY YOU SHELTER MANY

AMEN

DECREE:

YOU ARE A CHAMPION

YOU ARE SPECIAL

YOU ARE EQUIPPED

YOU ARE SMART

YOU ARE GOING PLACES

FACT:

FASTING IS HELPFUL

INSPIRATION:

KEEP IT FRESH

Destiny Come Forth

March 30

PRAYER:

MAY YOU BE REVIVED

MAY YOU REVIVE OTHERS

MAY YOU BELIEVE FOR GOD'S BEST

MAY YOU LISTEN ONLY TO THE GOOD NEWS

MAY YOU FOCUS ON THE BIG FINISH

AMEN

DECREE:

YOU READ THE WORD

YOU CONTINUE TO BE TRANSFORMED

YOU ARE LIT UP WITH THE GOOD NEWS

YOU ARE STRONG

YOU MAKE A DIFFERENCE

FACT:

FASTING BRINGS PEACE

INSPIRATION:

RUN WITH GOD

Destiny Come Forth

March 31

PRAYER:

MAY GOD MULTIPLY YOUR EFFORTS

MAY GOD OPEN DOORS FOR YOU

MAY GOD GIVE YOU COURAGE

MAY YOUR STRENGTH INCREASE

MAY YOU SEE VICTORY AFTER VICTORY

AMEN

DECREE:

YOU ARE SAVED

 YOU ARE FULL OF THE HOLY SPIRIT

YOU WALK IN TRUTH

YOU KNOW THE WAY

YOU LIVE THE LIFE GOD GAVE YOU

FACT:

FASTING FILLS THE TANK

INSPIRATION:

PRAY OUTSIDE THE LINES

April 1

PRAYER:

MAY THE WORDS OF GOD BUILD YOU UP

MAY YOU FIND RESTORATION

MAY YOU CONTINUE TO INCREASE

MAY YOU TAKE CARE OF EVERYTHING

MAY YOU BE RESPONSIBLE

AMEN

DECREE:

YOU ARE ABLE

YOU ARE FIERCE

YOU ARE STRONG IN GOD

YOU LOVE UNCONDITIONALLY

YOU BRING PEACE

FACT:

FASTING DIGNIFIES YOUR LIFE

INSPIRATION:

GO TO GOD

Destiny Come Forth

April 2

PRAYER:

MAY YOU GIVE GOD THE HONOR

MAY YOU HONOR HIS CREATION

MAY YOU WALK RELEVANTLY

MAY YOU CLEAN UP YOUR LIFE

MAY YOU SEEK PEACE

AMEN

DECREE:

YOUR LIFE LIGHTS UP THE WORLD

YOU BRING HEAVEN TO EARTH

GOD APPRECIATES YOUR EFFORT

YOU A MIGHTY

YOU ARE A MASTERPIECE

FACT:

FASTING IS REFRESHING

INSPIRATION:

LISTEN TO THE LORD WITH ALL YOUR HEART

Destiny Come Forth

April 3

PRAYER:

MAY YOU PROSPER

MAY YOU SOUND THE ALARM

MAY YOU WAKE UP YOUR PEOPLE

MAY YOU BE A GREAT LEADER

MAY YOU DEFY THE ODDS

AMEN

DECREE:

GOD TALKS TO YOU

YOU HEAR HIS WORDS

YOU LIVE VICARIOUSLY

HEAVEN SURROUNDS YOU

YOU ARE A GLORY BEARER

FACT:

FASTING BRINGS HEAVEN TO EARTH

INSPIRATION:

GOD HEARS

Destiny Come Forth

April 4

PRAYER:

MAY YOU BELIEVE IN GOD

MAY YOU TRUST GOD

MAY YOU LIVE A LIFE OF HONOR

MAY YOU THINK OF GOD ALL DAY LONG

MAY YOU PRESENT YOURSELF WELL

AMEN

DECREE:

YOU KEEP THE PACE

YOU FOLLOW THE WIND OF GOD

YOU FLOW

YOU ARE SENSITIVE

YOU ARE ON THE RIGHT TRACK

FACT:

FASTING BRINGS REWARDS

INSPIRATION:

SPEAKING IN TONGUES HELPS YOU CONTROL YOURS

Destiny Come Forth

April 5

PRAYER:

MAY YOU SEARCH FOR GOD'S TREASURE

MAY YOU FIND TREASURE IN OTHERS

MAY YOU POLISH UP HOLY GEMS

MAY YOU TAKE YOUR TIME

MAY YOU DO IT RIGHT

AMEN

DECREE:

YOU ARE A LIGHT

YOU LIGHT UP THE LIVES OF OTHERS

GOD SHINES THROUGH YOU

YOU BLESS THOSE AROUND YOU

YOU ARE BLESSED

FACT:

FASTING BRINGS FAVOR

INSPIRATION:

YOU MUST WEED YOUR SOUL

Destiny Come Forth

April 6

PRAYER:

MAY YOU FIND HAPPINESS IN WHAT YOU HAVE

MAY YOU LOOK AT ALL OF YOUR BLESSINGS

MAY YOU APPRECIATE THE GOOD, THE BAD, AND THE UGLY

MAY YOU LEARN TO LEARN FROM YOUR MISTAKES

MAY YOU BE REFRESHED TODAY

AMEN

DECREE:

YOU AMAZE OTHERS

YOUR ATTITUDE IS GREAT

YOU FIND THE GOOD IN EVERYTHING

YOU HAVE ENDURED THE UPS AND DOWNS OF LIFE WITH PERSEVERANCE

GOD LOVES THAT

FACT:

FASTING BURNS CALORIES FAST

INSPIRATION:

YOUR CORE SHOULD BE CHRIST

Destiny Come Forth

April 7

PRAYER:

MAY YOU ENJOY YOUR DAY

MAY YOU REMAIN IN A PLACE OF PEACE

MAY YOU STAY JOY FULL

THE JOY OF THE LORD IS YOUR STRENGTH

MAY YOU SHARE YOUR JOY

AMEN

DECREE:

YOU THANK GOD FOR THIS DAY

YOU HAVE WORKED HARD AND YOU HAVE PRAYED HARD

YOU GET SOME TIME TO REST

YOU KNOW THAT REST IS GOOD FOR YOU

YOU ENJOY IT

FACT:

FASTING EMPOWERS PRAYER

INSPIRATION:

KEEP YOUR EYES ON GOD

Destiny Come Forth

April 8

PRAYER:

MAY YOU ENJOY YOUR BLESSINGS

MAY YOU ENJOY YOUR MIRACLES

MAY YOUR FAITH INCREASE

MAY YOU STEP OUT IN FAITH

MAY YOU PULL ON GOD

AMEN

DECREE:

YOU MOVE ON

YOU TESTIFY

YOU BRING BREAKTHROUGH

YOU REJOICE

YOU KEEP YOUR EYES ON GOD

FACT:

FASTING SPEEDS THINGS UP

INSPIRATION:

GOD DOES GREAT THINGS FOR YOU

Destiny Come Forth

April 9

PRAYER:

MAY YOU FOLLOW GOD

MAY YOU HEAR THE GOOD NEWS

MAY YOU FOCUS ON YOUR HEART

MAY YOU TUNE IN TO VICTORY

MAY YOU REJOICE WITH OTHERS

AMEN

DECREE:

YOU ARE SOLID

YOU ARE FLEXIBLE

YOU ARE FULL OF JOY

YOU ARE HEALTHY

YOU ARE VIGOROUS

FACT:

FASTING IS A STABILIZING FORCE

INSPIRATION:

MOVE WITH AUTHORITY

Destiny Come Forth

April 10

PRAYER:

MAY YOU FIND STRENGTH TO MOVE

MAY EVERY DAY BE A JOYOUS JOURNEY

MAY YOUR MOMENTUM GAIN

MAY GOD'S GRACE EMPOWER YOU

MAY YOU WALK THE DIVINE LINE

AMEN

DECREE:

JOY IS YOUR WAY

YOU LIGHT UP THE WORLD

YOU ARE A PEACEMAKER

YOU LOOK FOR LOVE

YOU ARE GOOD

FACT:

FASTING GUIDES YOUR LIFE

INSPIRATION:

SHINE LIKE JESUS

Destiny Come Forth

April 11

PRAYER:

MAY YOU FIND STRENGTH IN GOD

MAY YOU STAY IN GOD'S PRESENCE

MAY YOU OWN UP

MAY YOU SHOW UP WITH HOPE

MAY YOU BRING JOY

AMEN

DECREE:

YOU ARE STRONG

YOU ARE HEALTHY

YOU TAKE GOOD CARE OF YOUR MIND

YOU THINK GOOD THOUGHTS

YOU PONDER THE THINGS OF GOD

FACT:

FASTING BRINGS JOY

INSPIRATION:

LOVE IS BETTER THAN HATE

Destiny Come Forth

April 12

PRAYER:

MAY YOU HAVE A GREAT DAY

MAY YOU SPREAD THE LOVE

MAY YOU WALK IN PEACE

MAY YOU HEAR GOD SPEAK

MAY YOU TESTIFY

AMEN

DECREE:

YOU LOVE WHAT GOD SAYS

YOU ARE AMAZED BY HIS PRESENCE

YOU SHARE THE JOY OF THE LORD

YOU GIVE CHRISTIANITY A GOOD NAME

YOU GATHER TOGETHER

FACT:

FASTING SETS YOUR MIND ON CHRIST

INSPIRATION:

WALK WITH JESUS EVERYDAY

Destiny Come Forth

April 13

PRAYER:

MAY YOU SEE THE LIGHT OF GOD

MAY YOU WALK WITH GOD DAILY

MAY YOU STAY IN THE SHELTER OF THE ALMIGHTY

MAY YOU TAKE CARE OF THE THINGS OF GOD

MAY YOU BE A TRUSTWORTHY SERVANT

AMEN

DECREE:

YOUR FAMILY COUNTS ON YOU

YOU SAY HOPE FULL

YOU PERSEVERE

YOU ARE TRIUMPHANT

YOUR FAITH HELPS PEOPLE DREAM

FACT:

FASTING FINDS FAVOR

INSPIRATION:

FILL YOURSELF WITH THE LOVE OF GOD

Destiny Come Forth

April 14

PRAYER:

MAY YOU OBEY GOD

MAY YOUR MIND, WILL, AND EMOTIONS LINE UP

MAY YOU TAKE GOOD CARE OF YOUR BODY

MAY YOUR SPIRIT SOAR

MAY YOU INSPIRE OTHERS

AMEN

DECREE:

YOU TAKE HEED

YOU HEAR THE WORDS OF GOD

YOU WALK IN THE TRUTH

YOU KNOW THE WAYS OF GOD

YOU HELP OTHER PEOPLE

FACT:

FASTING GETS YOU CLOSER TO GOD

INSPIRATION:

DO GOOD FOR OTHERS

April 15

PRAYER:

MAY YOU RUN WITH GOD

MAY YOU RUN WITH GOD'S FAMILY

MAY YOU RUN WITH LOVE

MAY YOU DANCE IN VICTORY

MAY YOU ENJOY YOUR REWARD

AMEN

DECREE:

YOU RUN INTO THE DAY WITH HOPE

YOU LOVE GOD WITH ALL YOUR HEART

YOU SERVE GOD WITH FORTITUDE

YOU LOVE PEOPLE

YOU LAY YOUR LIFE DOWN WILLINGLY

FACT:

FASTING TAKES COURAGE

INSPIRATION:

GOD HEARS YOUR PRAYERS

April 16

PRAYER:

MAY YOU FIND YOUR STRENGTH IN THE LORD

MAY YOU REMIND OTHERS WHERE THEIR HELP COMES FROM

MAY YOU STRENGTHEN EACH OTHER

MAY YOU YOKE UP

MAY YOU MOVE FORWARD IN UNITY

AMEN

DECREE:

YOU ARE HEADED TOWARD VICTORY

YOU ARE LEADING THE WAY

YOU MAKE A BIG DIFFERENCE

YOU TRY HARD

YOU NEVER GIVE UP

FACT:

FASTING HEALS YOUR BODY

INSPIRATION:

WALK LIKE JESUS

April 17

PRAYER:

MAY YOU RISE UP

MAY YOU STAY UP

MAY YOU HELP OTHER PEOPLE UP

MAY YOU GET YOUR LIFT FROM GOD

MAY YOU SHARE YOUR STRENGTH

AMEN

DECREE:

YOU HAVE RESURRECTION POWER INSIDE OF YOU

YOU LOOK FOR OPPORTUNITIES TO RELEASE GOD'S POWER

YOUR FAITH HAS GOTTEN EVEN STRONGER

MOUNTAINS MOVE FOR YOU

YOU ARE ANOINTED

FACT:

FASTING PRODUCES A REFUGE

INSPIRATION:

FOCUS ON WHAT'S POSITIVE

Destiny Come Forth

April 18

PRAYER:

MAY YOUR LIFE LOOK LIKE CHRISTS

MAY YOU LAY YOUR LIFE DOWN FOR EVERYONE

MAY THE KINDNESS OF GOD FLOW THROUGH YOU

MAY YOU THINK OF OTHER PEOPLE FIRST

MAY YOU FEEL VALUED BY GOD

AMEN

DECREE:

YOU RADIATE THE LOVE OF GOD

THE LOVE OF GOD COMPELS YOU

YOU DO WHAT IS RIGHT

YOU ARE LED BY GOD'S HOLY SPIRIT

YOU ARE OPEN FOR DIVINE APPOINTMENTS

FACT:

FASTING INDUCES GOD'S POWER

INSPIRATION:

THERE IS NOTHING TOO HARD FOR GOD

Destiny Come Forth

April 19

PRAYER:

MAY YOU LIVE A LIFE OF STRONG FAITH

MAY YOUR FAITH CONTINUE TO GROW

MAY YOU SHARE YOUR FAITH CONTINUALLY

MAY YOU DECREE THE GOODNESS OF GOD

MAY YOU PRAY BOLDLY

MAY YOUR SURROUND YOURSELF WITH PRAYER WARRIORS

AMEN

DECREE:

YOU ARE FULL OF ENERGY

YOU GET THE JOB DONE

YOU HELP OTHER PEOPLE ACCOMPLISH EXPLOITS

YOU ARE SUPPORTIVE

YOU BRING THE RESOURCES OF HEAVEN TO EARTH

FACT:

FASTING STRENGTHENS YOUR FAITH

INSPIRATION:

BE FULL OF ENCOURAGEMENT AND EXPLODE EVERYWHERE YOU GO

Destiny Come Forth

April 20

PRAYER:

MAY YOU GO INTO THE DAY WITH JOY

MEY YOU SHARE YOUR HOPE WITH THE WORLD

MAY YOU BE A SOURCE OF ENCOURAGEMENT

MAY YOU BE A SOURCE OF JOY

MAY YOU BRING LIFE TO THE PARTY

AMEN

DECREE:

YOU ARE AN OVERCOMER

YOU HELP OTHER PEOPLE OVERCOME

YOU LIFT PEOPLE UP

GOD GIVES YOU SUPERNATURAL STRENGTH

YOU GLOW FORTH

FACT:

FASTING REFUELS YOUR HEART

INSPIRATION:

VALUE THE GIFTS IN OTHERS

Destiny Come Forth

April 21

PRAYER:

MAY YOU BE GUIDED BY GOD

MAY YOU LISTEN CLOSELY TO GOD'S WORDS

MAY YOU SHARE WHAT YOU HEAR

MAY YOU BE A BLESSING TO OTHERS

MAY YOU LOVE OTHERS WELL

AMEN

DECREE:

YOU DECLARE VICTORY

YOU DEMAND JUSTICE

YOU CLING TO GOD

YOU LIVE IN FREEDOM

YOU STAY STOUT

FACT:

FASTING PUTS GOOD FUEL IN YOUR TANK

INSPIRATION:

BE EXTRAORDINARY

April 22

PRAYER:

MAY YOU LOVE THE LORD WITH ALL YOUR HEART

MAY YOU UNDERSTAND GOD WITH ALL YOUR MIND

MAY YOU CONTINUE TO LEARN

MAY YOU EXPAND UPWARD

MAY YOU RISE WITH EXCELLENCE

AMEN

DECREE:

GOD PROTECTS YOU

GOD GUIDES YOU

GOD LOVES TO HEAR YOU LAUGH

GOD HAS MADE A WAY FOR YOU

GOD STICKS BY YOU

FACT:

FASTING FINDS TRUTH

INSPIRATION:

FILL YOUR SPIRIT WITH GOD'S HOLY SPIRIT

Destiny Come Forth

April 23

PRAYER:

MAY YOU LOOK TO GOD TODAY

MAY YOU HEAR FROM GOD

MAY YOU DO WHAT GOD SAYS

MAY YOU BE KIND-HEARTED LIKE GOD

MAY YOU USE YOUR GOD GIVEN AUTHORITY

AMEN

DECREE:

YOU ARE LEARNING MORE AND MORE EVERYDAY

YOUR BRAIN IS IN GOOD HEALTH

YOU TAKE GOOD CARE OF YOUR BODY

YOU CARE ABOUT OTHER PEOPLE

YOU ARE A GOOD PERSON

FACT:

FASTING MAKES YOUR PATH CLEAR

INSPIRATION:

THE ANOINTING IS THE POWER OF GOD

Destiny Come Forth

April 24

PRAYER:

MAY YOU LINE YOUR DAY UP WITH GOD

MAY YOU JOIN THE ARMY OF GOD

MAY YOU TRAIN HARD

MAY YOU PRACTICE DILIGENCE

MAY YOU PUSH THROUGH RESISTANCE

AMEN

DECREE:

YOU GIVE ALL

YOU ARE ALL IN

YOU ARE FOCUSED ON WHAT GOD WANTS

YOU LEAD WITH POWER

YOU FOLLOW WITH GRACE

FACT:

FASTING BRINGS HEAVEN'S POWER DOWN

INSPIRATION:

GOD LOVES YOU

Destiny Come Forth

April 25

PRAYER:

MAY YOU FEEL CONFIDENT

MAY YOU KNOW THAT GOD HAS YOUR BACK

MAY YOU UNDERSTAND YOUR WORTH

MAY YOUR STRENGTH INCREASE

MAY YOU FOLLOW GOD FORWARD

AMEN

DECREE:

YOU ARE BLESSED BY GOD

YOUR FAMILY AND FRIENDS BLESS YOU

NATURE CLAPS WHEN YOU WALK BY

YOU STEWARD THE ANOINTING WELL

YOU USE YOUR GIFTS TO BLESS YOUR TERRITORY

FACT:

FASTING IS A USEFUL TOOL

INSPIRATION:

LET GOD WORK THROUGH YOU

Destiny Come Forth

April 26

PRAYER:

MAY YOUR DAY PLEASE GOD

MAY YOU STAY IN LINE

MAY YOU LOOK TO GOD FOR GUIDANCE

MAY YOU LIVE RIGHT

MAY YOU GROW IN WISDOM

AMEN

DECREE:

THE POWER OF GOD SURROUNDS YOU

YOU BRING FREEDOM TO THE EARTH

YOU WALK INTO VICTORY

THE BIBLE IS YOUR BLUEPRINT

YOU STUDY THE PLANS OF GOD

FACT:

FASTING OPENS YOUR EARS TO HEAR GOD

INSPIRATION:

WHEN YOU ARE ON UNCHARTED WATERS YOU JUST HAVE TO GO FOR IT

Destiny Come Forth

April 27

PRAYER:

MAY YOU TURN THE OTHER CHEEK

MAY YOU GIVE MORE THAN YOU OWE

MAY YOU WALK BLAMELESSLY

MAY YOU FORGIVE YOURSELF DAILY AS GOD DOES

MAY YOU ENJOY YOUR PEACE

AMEN

DECREE:

YOU ARE SERIOUS ABOUT YOUR FRIENDS

EVERYONE MATTERS TO YOU

YOUR GIFTS AND TALENTS SHINE

YOU MAKE THE MOST OF WHAT YOU HAVE

YOUR LIFESTYLE IS A BEACON

FACT:

FASTING REVEALS DEPTH

INSPIRATION:

GOD LOVES TO HELP US

Destiny Come Forth

April 28

PRAYER:

MAY YOU RUN INTO YOUR DAY

MAY YOU GO TO CHURCH TO BE A BLESSING

MAY YOU INVITE YOUR LOVED ONES

MAY YOU CARE ABOUT ETERNITY

MAY YOU GET LOUD WITH LOVE

AMEN

DECREE:

GOD GUIDES YOU

YOU HAVE WISDOM PLUS ZEAL

YOU CONTINUE TO LEARN AND GROW

THE WORLD IS BEFORE YOU

NO REGRETS

FACT:

FASTING RELIEVES STRESS

INSPIRATION:

IF ALL WE DO AS CHRISTIANS IS HANG AROUND WITH OTHER CHRISTIANS WE ARE NOT DOING

OUR CHRISTIAN PART

Destiny Come Forth

April 29

PRAYER;

MAY YOU BE AT PEACE

MAY YOU EARNESTLY SEEK TO BE LOVING

MAY YOU FORGIVE YOURSELF WHEN YOU FALL SHORT

MAY YOU RECEIVE THE GRACE OF GOD

MAY YOU KNOW YOU ARE UNDER THE SHELTER OF THE ALMIGHTY

AMEN

DECREE:

YOU ARE READY FOR THE DAY

YOU ENJOY YOUR TIME OFF

YOU LOVE TO GATHER WITH YOUR CHURCH FAMILY AND FRIENDS

YOU TAKE TIME TO REST

YOU PLAY HARD

FACT:

FASTING IS WORTH THE EFFORT

INSPIRATION:

PUT GOD FIRST

Destiny Come Forth

April 30

PRAYER:

MAY YOU HEAR FROM GOD

MAY YOU ENJOY HIS PRESENCE

MAY YOU SHARE HIS LOVE

MAY YOU RESEMBLE GOD

MAY YOU CARRY ON HIS NAME

AMEN

DECREE:

YOU ARE WORTHWHILE

YOU MATTER

GOD KNOWS EVERYTHING ABOUT YOU

YOUR GOOD DEEDS ARE NOTICED

YOU ARE LOVED

FACT:

FASTING SERVES GOD

INSPIRATION:

GOD HAS YOUR DESTINY IN HIS HANDS

Destiny Come Forth

May 1

PRAYER:

MAY YOUR LIFE EXALT GOD

MAY YOUR LEGACY LIVE ON

MAY YOUR MOVEMENT CAUSE A RIPPLING EFFECT

MAY JOY SURROUND YOU

MAY YOU STAY BRAVE

AMEN

DECREE:

YOU ARE IN THE MOOD TO CELEBRATE

YOU CAN FEEL THE JOY OF HEAVEN ON EARTH

YOU KNOW GOD IS PROUD OF YOU

YOU REJOICE WITH OTHERS

YOU HAVE GREAT FRIENDS

FACT:

FASTING IS A ROTOTILLER

INSPIRATION:

WE CAN FORGIVE BECAUSE GOD FORGAVE US FIRST

Destiny Come Forth

May 2

PRAYER:

YOU HAVE GOOD INTENTIONS

YOUR THOUGHTS ARE CLEAR

YOU ARE GUIDED BY GOD

YOU KEEP THINGS PLAIN AND SIMPLE

YOUR HEART IS PURE

AMEN

DECREE:

YOU ARE GLORIOUS

YOU ARE FILLED WITH THE LIVING GOD

YOU BRING GOOD NEWS

YOU SPEAK VICTORIOUS WORDS

BREAKTHROUGH IS ON EVERY SIDE

FACT:

FASTING BRINGS OUT THE GOOD IN YOU

INSPIRATION:

SEEK GOD

Destiny Come Forth

May 3

PRAYER:

MAY YOU SURRENDER YOUR LIFE TO GOD COMPLETELY

MAY YOU BE A LIVING EXAMPLE OF RIGHTEOUSNESS

MAY YOUR FAMILY LINE BE BLESSED BY YOU

MAY YOU BRING FORTH POSITIVE CHANGE

MAY YOU BREAK INTO HEAVEN ON EARTH

AMEN

DECREE:

YOU ARE A SOLDIER IN THE ARMY OF THE LORD

YOU SERVE GOD WELL

YOU DEFEND THE RIGHTS OF OTHERS

YOU ARE ON DUTY

YOUR MISSION IS IN GOD'S HANDS

FACT:

FASTING STARTS REVIVAL

INSPIRATION:

JESUS SHINES THROUGH YOU

May 4

PRAYER:

MAY YOU FAST AND PRAY REGULARLY

MAY YOU MAKE A BIG DIFFERENCE

MAY YOU WALK WITH GOD

MAY YOU CONTINUE TO LEARN

MAY YOU TAKE TIME TO STUDY

AMEN

DECREE:

YOU ARE FULL OF HOPE

YOU ARE FULL OF JOY

YOU ARE FULL OF LOVE

YOU ARE FULL OF PEACE

YOU ARE HEAVENLY

FACT:

FASTING REACHES GOD

INSPIRATION:

REALIZE THE LOVE OF GOD IN YOU

Destiny Come Forth

May 5

PRAYER:

MAY YOU SURRENDER YOUR LIFE TO GOD COMPLETELY

MAY YOU BE A LIVING EXAMPLE OF RIGHTEOUSNESS

MAY YOUR FAMILY LINE BE BLESSED BY YOU

MAY YOU BRING FORTH POSITIVE CHANGE

MAY YOU BREAK INTO HEAVEN ON EARTH

AMEN

DECREE:

YOU WALK IN FORGIVENESS

YOU HAVE BEEN FORGIVEN AND YOU FORGIVE OTHERS

YOU LIFE IS FULL OF GOD'S LOVE

YOU ARE GRACIOUS

YOU ENJOY YOUR TIME WITH GOD

FACT:

FASTING IS GOOD WORK

INSPIRATION:

JUST THANK GOD

Destiny Come Forth

May 6

PRAYER:

MAY YOU FOLLOW GOD'S PLAN

MAY YOU HELP OTHER PEOPLE FIND THE WILL OF GOD

MAY YOU SURRENDER WITH YOUR LIFE

MAY YOU CARE ABOUT WHAT GOD WANTS

MAY YOU CARE FOR OTHER PEOPLE

AMEN

DECREE:

YOU LOVE GOD

YOU LOVE PEOPLE

YOU LOVE LIFE

YOU TAKE GOOD CARE OF THE EARTH

YOU TREAT ANIMALS WITH KINDNESS

FACT:

FASTING PREPARES THE WAY

INSPIRATION:

SITTING WITH THE LORD SHARPENS YOUR SWORD

Destiny Come Forth

May 7

PRAYER:

MAY YOU ENJOY YOUR DAY

MAY YOU BE FILLED WITH GOD'S PEACE

MAY YOU OVERFLOW WITH EXPECTATION

MAY YOU PUSH AHEAD

MAY YOUR TRAIL REMAIN

AMEN

DECREE:

YOU ARE FULL OF LOVE

YOU OVERFLOW

YOU POUR YOURSELF OUT EVERYWHERE YOU GO

YOU SERVE

YOU GIVE EVERYTHING

FACT:

FASTING HEALS YOUR HEART

INSPIRATION:

STAY CLOSE TO GOD

Destiny Come Forth

May 8

PRAYER:

MAY YOU EAT HEALTHY

MAY YOU BE A GOOD EXAMPLE

MAY YOU TAKE CARE OF YOURSELF

MAY YOU GET PLENTY OF REST

MAY YOU HAVE FUN

AMEN

DECREE:

YOU ARE HAPPY

YOU ARE FUN

YOU ARE SWEET

YOU ARE PURE

YOU ARE A TRUE DISCIPLE OF JESUS

FACT:

FASTING IS A PIPELINE TO HEAVEN

INSPIRATION:

BE LIKE CHRIST AND OPEN YOUR MIND

Destiny Come Forth

May 9

PRAYER:

MAY YOU RISE TO THE TOP

MAY YOU KEEP YOUR EYES ON GOD

MAY YOU BE A GREAT EXAMPLE

MAY YOUR CHARACTER CONTINUE TO DEVELOP

MAY THE PRAYERS FOR YOUR LEGACY BE ANSWERED

AMEN

DECREE:

YOU WATCH WHAT YOU SAY

YOU THINK THINGS THROUGH

YOU SUBMIT EVERYTHING TO GOD

YOU GLADLY OBEY

YOU LOVE SERVING

FACT:

FASTING ANSWERS PRAYERS

INSPIRATION:

GOD IS ALWAYS LISTENING BUT ARE YOU?

Destiny Come Forth

May 9

PRAYER:

MAY YOU HIT THE MARK

MAY YOU GO WHERE GOD SENDS YOU

MAY YOU DO WHAT GOD ASKS YOU TO DO

MAY YOU STAY STRONG

MAY YOU BE VERY COURAGEOUS

AMEN

DECREE:

YOU ARE QUALIFIED

GOD IS ON YOU

YOU MOVE FORWARD

YOU TAKE GROUND

YOU GIVE ALL

FACT:

FASTING BRINGS REVELATION

INSPIRATION:

LISTEN TO GOD AND HE WILL SPEAK

Destiny Come Forth

May 10

PRAYER:

MAY YOU KEEP GOD FIRST IN YOUR LIFE

MAY YOU BE CONTENT

MAY YOU BE THANKFUL

MAY YOU HEAR GOD

MAY YOU OBEY GOD

AMEN

DECREE:

YOU KEEP THINGS LIGHT

YOU SHINE UPWARD AND OUTWARD

YOU ALWAYS LOOK FOR WAYS TO HELP

YOU STEWARD YOUR TIME WELL

YOU ARE EXCITED

FACT:

FASTING PLEASES GOD

INSPIRATION:

A LOT OF THINGS HAVE TIMING SO WAIT FOR IT

Destiny Come Forth

May 11

PRAYER:

MAY YOU SERVE GOD

MAY YOU SERVE PEOPLE

MAY YOU GIVE WHAT YOU CAN GIVE

MAY YOU LAY YOUR LIFE DOWN

MAY THE JOY OF THE LORD BE YOUR JOY

AMEN

DECREE:

YOU KEEP YOUR HEAD DOWN WHEN YOU ARE WORKING

YOU FOCUS ON THE TIME AT HAND

YOU ARE A FINISHER

YOU SUCCEED

YOU ACCOMPLISH MANY GREAT THINGS

FACT:

FASTING OPENS YOUR MIND

INSPIRATION:

GOD IS ALWAYS UP TO SOMETHING

Destiny Come Forth

May 12

PRAYER:

MAY YOU FIND STRENGTH

MAY YOUR HOPE BE ENCOURAGED

MAY YOU BELIEVE FOR BREAKTHROUGH

MAY YOU PUSH INTO GOD

MAY YOU FOCUS ON THE GOOD NEWS

AMEN

DECREE:

YOU ARE GLOWING

YOU ARE FULL OF GOOD NEWS

YOU ARE BURSTING WITH JOY

YOU HAVE BEEN REFRESHED

YOU ARE READY FOR THIS DAY

FACT:

FASTING PURSUES CHRIST

INSPIRATION:

GOD COMES THROUGH

Destiny Come Forth

May 13

PRAYER:

MAY YOU KEEP YOUR HEAD

MAY YOU REACH TO GOD

MAY YOU LET GOD LEAD

MAY YOU FOLLOW GOD EVER SO CLOSELY

MAY YOU KEEP UP

AMEN

DECREE:

GOD TALKS TO YOU

YOU SHARE WHAT GOD SAYS

YOU HONOR GOD

YOU RESPECT OTHER PEOPLE

YOU ARE A GENUINE PERSON

FACT:

FASTING BRINGS YOU CLOSER TO GOD

INSPIRATION:

HOPE TO YOUR MIND NOW

Destiny Come Forth

May 14

PRAYER:

MAY YOU WALK RIGHT

MAY YOU STAND TALL

MAY YOU SPEAK BLESSINGS

MAY YOU HELP YOUR NEIGHBOR

MAY YOU STAY STRONG

AMEN

DECREE:

YOU ARE FULL OF HOPE

YOU ENCOURAGE EVERYONE YOU MEET

YOU ARE SUCH A GOOD EXAMPLE

YOU LEAVE A BRIGHT TRAIL TO FOLLOW

EVERYONE THANKS YOU

FACT:

FASTING STIRS UP YOUR SPIRIT

INSPIRATION:

SOME PEOPLE NEVER CHANGE BUT DON'T LET THAT STOP YOU

Destiny Come Forth

May 15

PRAYER:

MAY YOU BREAK THE CURSE

MAY YOU TEACH OTHERS TO ACHIEVE FREEDOM

MAY YOU CONTINUE TO LEARN AS YOU TEACH

MAY YOU THRIVE IN THE HOUSE OF GOD

MAY YOUR FAITH CONTINUE TO INCREASE

AMEN

DECREE:

YOU HAVE FOUND THE RHYTHM OF HEAVEN

YOU GO WITH THE FLOW

YOU MOVE WITH GOD'S GRACE

YOU ONLY DO WHAT GOD ASKS YOU TO DO

YOU ARE FAITH FULL

FACT:

FASTING REVITALIZES YOUR CELLS

INSPIRATION:

YOU HAVE TO START SOMEWHERE SO START

Destiny Come Forth

May 16

PRAYER:

MAY YOU BE MORE LOVING EVERY DAY

MAY YOU LOOK TO GOD FOR STRENGTH

MAY YOU LOOK TO JESUS AS AN EXAMPLE

MAY YOU FOCUS ON THE BEST

MAY YOU HELP OTHER PEOPLE FOCUS

AMEN

DECREE:

YOU HEAL FAST

YOU RISE ABOVE OPPOSITION

YOU TURN THE OTHER CHEEK

THE LOVE INSIDE OF YOU IS STRONGER THAN THE WORLD'S HATRED

YOU ARE A LOVE EPISTLE

FACT:

FASTING IS A DISCIPLINE

INSPIRATION:

LOOK AHEAD

Destiny Come Forth

May 17

PRAYER:

MAY YOU SHARE WHAT YOU KNOW

MAY YOU EXPAND YOUR TERRITORY

MAY YOU TRY HARD TO REACH THE LOST

MAY YOU BE BRAVE THIS WEEK

MAY YOU USE YOUR GIFTS AND TALENTS WISELY

AMEN

DECREE:

YOU ARE HEARTY

YOU DO MORE THAN YOUR SHARE

GOD TRUSTS YOU

GOD GIVES YOU JOBS TO DO

YOU DO THEM WELL

FACT:

FASTING PARTNERS WITH PRAYER

INSPIRATION:

RUN INTO THE FAMILY OF GOD

Destiny Come Forth

May 18

PRAYER:

MAY YOU SERVE GOD

MAY YOU SERVE PEOPLE

MAY YOU SERVE IN THE CHURCH

MAY YOU SERVE IN YOUR COMMUNITY

MAY YOU SERVE IN OUR COUNTRY

AMEN

DECREE:

YOUR PATIENCE IS A VIRTUE

YOU ARE GOD'S BELOVED CHILD

YOU DO THE RIGHT THINGS

YOU STAY FULL OF THE POWER OF GOD

YOU ARE A BLESSING

FACT:

FASTING IS HOLY DANCING

INSPIRATION:

TAP INTO GOD'S GOODNESS

Destiny Come Forth

May 19

PRAYER:

MAY YOU ENJOY YOUR DAY

MAY YOU SPEND QUALITY TIME WITH FAMILY AND FRIENDS

MAY YOU SEEK GOD'S BEST

MAY YOU TAKE TIME TO STUDY GOD'S WORD

MAY YOU ENHANCE YOUR CHURCH FAMILY

AMEN

DECREE:

YOU ARE VICTORIOUS

YOU WILL WIN AND WIN AND WIN

YOU CHOOSE HOLINESS

YOU SHARE THE GOSPEL

YOU ARE ON FIRE WITH LOVE

FACT:

FASTING WILL HELP YOU

INSPIRATION:

STRIVE FOR THE BEST

Destiny Come Forth

May 20

PRAYER:

MAY YOU SEE THE SILVER LINING

MAY YOU COME UP AS PURE GOLD

MAY THE WISDOM OF GOD SURROUND YOU

MAY YOU LIVE IN THE RIGHT TIME

MAY YOU ECHO HEAVEN

AMEN

DECREE:

YOU KEEP MOVING FORWARD

YOU MAKE THE MOST OUT OF EVERY MOMENT

YOU ARE SUNSHINE

YOU GLOW WITH GOD'S GOODNESS

YOU BEAM HIGH

FACT:

FASTING FUELS YOUR SPIRIT

INSPIRATION:

DO THE RIGHT THINGS

Destiny Come Forth

May 21

PRAYER:

MAY YOU HEAR THE LORD TODAY

MAY YOU BE ENCOURAGED

MAY YOU FIGHT FOR WHAT IS RIGHT

MAY YOU HELP YOUR NEIGHBOR

MAY YOU BE A GOOD EXAMPLE

AMEN

DECREE:

YOU ARE STRONG HEARTED

YOUR FAITH PUSHES YOU

YOU HEAR THE TRUTH

YOU DO THE RIGHT THINGS

YOU ARE ALL IN

FACT:

FASTING IS A GREAT START TO YOUR DAY

INSPIRATION:

LOVE LIKE JESUS DOES

Destiny Come Forth

May 22

PRAYER:

MAY YOUR HEART BE GLAD

MAY YOU BE CONTENT TO DO YOUR BEST

MAY YOU LOVE TO HELP

MAY YOU SERVE EVERYONE

MAY YOU LAY DOWN YOUR LIFE

AMEN

DECREE:

YOU HAVE LEARNED A LOT

YOU APPLY WHAT YOU NEED TO KNOW

YOU MAKE THE MOST OUT OF LIFE

YOU ARE SWEET TO THE SOUL

YOU HAVE BEEN FOUND FAITHFUL

FACT:

FASTING BRINGS JOY

INSPIRATION:

YOU CAN RESPECT THOSE THAT DO NOT RESPECT YOU

Destiny Come Forth

May 23

PRAYER:

MAY YOU WALK UPRIGHT

MAY YOU DO WHAT IS RIGHT

MAY YOU UNDERSTAND THE TRUTH

MAY YOU TELL THE TRUTH

MAY YOU WALK WITH GOD TODAY

AMEN

DECREE:

INTEGRITY IS INGRAINED IN YOU

YOU HAVE TO BE HONEST

YOU WALK IN THE LIGHT THAT GOD PROVIDES

YOU ARE SAFE

OUR HEART IS A POOL OF REFRESHMENT

FACT:

FASTING OPENS YOUR HEART TO GOD

INSPIRATION:

TRUST GOD COMPLETELY

Destiny Come Forth

May 24

PRAYER:

MAY YOU RUN WITH GOD

MAY YOU JUMP INTO THE FATHER'S ARMS

MAY YOU BELIEVE WHAT HE SAYS ABOUT YOU

MAY YOU HOLD YOUR HEAD HIGH

MAY YOU ACHIEVE YOUR DREAMS

AMEN

DECREE::

YOU ARE AMAZING

YOU SHINE WITH GOD'S LOVE

YOU ARE GREAT TO BE AROUND

YOU CHANGE HEARTS

YOU ARE A POSITIVE INFLUENCE

FACT:

FASTING ENHANCES YOUR GIFTINGS

INSPIRATION:

GOD HOLDS YOU

Destiny Come Forth

May 25

PRAYER:

MAY YOU SEEK REFUGE IN GOD

MAY YOU BE LOYAL

MAY YOU BE TENDER HEARTED

MAY YOU SHINE WIDE

MAY YOUR LOVE EXPAND

AMEN

DECREE:

YOU FOCUS ON THE RIGHT THINGS

YOU KEEP THINGS CLEAR

YOU PRAISE GOD

YOU INHABIT HEAVEN

YOU BRING LOVE TO EARTH

FACT:

FASTING OPENS UP HEAVEN

INSPIRATION:

GOD WANTS YOU TO WIN

Destiny Come Forth

May 26

PRAYER:

MAY YOU STOP AND LISTEN

MAY YOUR HEART BE FILLED

MAY YOU REAP WHAT YOU SOW

MAY YOU LOVE YOUR LIFE

MAY YOU ENJOY YOUR DAY

AMEN

DECREE:

GOD SPEAKS TO YOU

YOU HEAR GOD CLEARLY

YOUR FAITH IS STRONG

YOU ACCOMPLISH THE WILL OF GOD

ETERNAL LIFE IS YOUR LEGACY

FACT:

FASTING FREES UP TIME

INSPIRATION:

MAKE A JOY FILLED NOISE

Destiny Come Forth

May 27

PRAYER:

MAY YOU WIN THE RACE

MAY YOU RUN FULL STEAM AHEAD

MAY YOU KEEP YOUR FOOTING

MAY YOU CLIMB TO THE TOP

MAY YOU ROLL WITH GOD

AMEN

DECREE:

YOU ARE A PREACHING MACHINE

YOU ARE REVVED UP

YOU FLOOR IT

YOU GO PLACES

YOU LIGHT UP A TRAIL

FACT:

FASTING KEEP YOU ON THE RIGHT PATH

INSPIRATION:

ENCOURAGE THOSE TRYING TO MAKE A DIFFERENCE

Destiny Come Forth

May 28

PRAYER:

MAY YOUR HEART BE FULL

MAY YOUR LIFE BE LONG

MAY YOU BE REJUVENATED

MAY YOUR YOUTH BE RESTORED

MAY YOU ALWAYS LOOK TO GOD

AMEN

DECREE:

YOU HAVE WISDOM

YOU WILL NOT APOLOGIZE FOR THE GIFTS OF GOD

YOU ARE FULL OF THE HOLY SPIRIT

YOU ARE HERE TO HELP OTHER PEOPLE

YOU ARE WELL RECEIVED

FACT:

FASTING OPENS DOORS

INSPIRATION:

TURN YOUR EYES TO HEAVEN

Destiny Come Forth

May 29

PRAYER:

MAY ALL OF YOUR GOOD DEEDS COME BACK TO GET YOU

MAY YOUR REWARD IMPACT GENERATIONS

MAY YOU HONOR GOD

MAY YOU HONOR THOSE IN MILITARY

MAY YOU FIGHT THE GOOD FIGHT OF FAITH

AMEN

DECREE:

YOU ARE MILITANT

YOU FAITH INCREASES DAY BY DAY

YOU ARE STRONG

YOU ARE HEALTHY

YOU HAVE GOD WITH YOU

FACT:

FASTING REDIRECTS YOUR ATTENTION

INSPIRATION:

BELIEVE FOR THE IMPOSSIBLE AND DO IT

Destiny Come Forth

May 30

PRAYER:

MAY YOU DETERMINE TO BE THANK FULL

MAY YOU REALIZE HOW BLESSED YOU ARE

MAY YOU CONTINUE TO COUNT ON GOD

MAY YOU BE COUNTED ON

MAY YOU APPRECIATE YOUR OPPORTUNITIES TO LOVE MORE

AMEN

DECREE:

YOU ARE WARM AND FRIENDLY

PEOPLE CAN GET NEXT TO YOU

YOU HAVE FOUND FAVOR WITH GOD AND PEOPLE

YOU ARE RADIANT

YOUR INSTINCTS ARE HONED INTO WHAT GOD WANTS

FACT:

FASTING INTERRUPTS LETHARGY

INSPIRATION:

ILLUMINATE THE BEST

Destiny Come Forth

May 31

PRAYER:

MAY YOU REACH UP TO WHAT GOD WANTS FOR YOU

MAY YOU BRING IT HERE

MAY YOU STOP ALL COMPLAINING AND MURMURING

MAY YOU USE YOUR WORDS TO HEAL

MAY YOU SPEAK LIFE

AMEN

DECREE:

YOU TAKE TIME AND MAKE IT BEHAVE

YOU MAKE UP FOR LOST TIME

YOU FOLLOW GOD'S PLAN FOR YOUR LIFE

YOU DO NOTHING MORE AND NOTHING LESS

YOU ARE AN ENCOURAGER

FACT:

FASTING BUILDS A THRESHOLD

INSPIRATION:

PRAYER IS POWER AUTHORITY

Destiny Come Forth

June 1

PRAYER:

MAY YOU HEAR THE VOICE OF GOD

MAY YOU FOLLOW GOD WITH YOUR LIFESTYLE

MAY YOU TEACH AND TRAIN OTHER PEOPLE

MAY YOU HIT THE BULLSEYE

MAY YOUR LIFE CLAP

AMEN

DECREE:

YOU ARE MORE THAN ENOUGH

YOU ACCOMPLISH GREAT THINGS

GOD IS PROUD OF YOU

YOU ARE COMPLETE

YOU ARE ALWAYS READY FOR MORE

FACT:

FASTING ENHANCES THE VOICE OF GOD

INSPIRATION:

PUSH INTO GOD

Destiny Come Forth

June 2

PRAYER:

MAY YOU FIND YOURSELF

MAY GOD SHOW YOU WHO YOU ARE

MAY YOU REMEMBER YOUR PART

MAY YOU STAY SOLID

MAY YOU BUILD ON GOD'S FOUNDATION

AMEN

DECREE:

YOU TAP INTO GOD

YOU DON'T EVER HAVE TO BE AFRAID

YOU ARE ROYALTY

GOD HAS SET YOU UP

YOU WALK RIGHT INTO YOUR DESTINY

FACT:

FASTING GROWS YOUR FAITH

INSPIRATION:

PRAY FERVENTLY

June 3

PRAYER:

MAY YOU FIND PEACE

MAY YOU FIND JOY

MAY YOU FIND HOPE

MAY YOU FIND REST

MAY YOU FIND LOVE

AMEN

DECREE:

YOU ARE FULL OF GOD'S LOVE

YOU EXUDE PATIENCE

MERCY IS YOUR MIDDLE NAME

YOU WIN OVER THE HARDEST OF HEARTS

YOU WEAR YOUR HEART ON YOUR SLEEVE

FACT:

FASTING FORMS A PIPELINE

INSPIRATION:

GOD LOVES US WITH ALL OF OUR IMPERFECTIONS

June 4

PRAYER:

MAY GOD HAVE MERCY ON YOU

MAY GOD HAVE MERCY ON US ALL

MAY GOD'S WILL BE DONE

MAY WE GET OUT OF THE WAY

MAY WE FOLLOW GOD TOGETHER

AMEN

DECREE:

YOU ARE A FORERUNNER

YOU RUN WITH ZEAL

YOU PIONEER

YOU BLAZE A PRAISE TRAIL

YOU HELP OTHERS GO FOR IT

FACT:

FASTING BRINGS OUT THE BEST IN EVERYONE

INSPIRATION:

BE GRATEFUL GOD IS GREAT

Destiny Come Forth

June 5

PRAYER:

MAY YOU EXPERIENCE BREAKTHROUGH

MAY YOU BE LEAD BY GOD

MAY YOU EXPERIENCE PERSONAL VICTORY

MAY YOU SHARE YOUR TESTIMONY

MAY YOU RISE UP WITH CONFIDENCE

AMEN

DECREE:

YOU ARE STRONG

YOU ARE SOLID

YOU ARE A RISING EDIFICE

THE TRUTH SETS YOUR FEET ON A FIRM FOUNDATION

GOD IS YOUR BUILDER

FACT:

FASTING INVITES THE HOLY SPIRIT IN

INSPIRATION:

GOD ANOINTS THE FAITHFUL

June 6

PRAYER:

MAY YOU BE CHERISHED

MAY YOU BE REMEMBERED

MAY YOU BE LOVED

MAY YOU FEEL ACCEPTED

MAY YOU LOVE YOURSELF

AMEN

DECREE:

YOU ARE MORE THAN ENOUGH

YOU ARE GOOD ENOUGH

GOD THINKS YOU ARE GREAT

YOU ARE MADE WHOLE IN CHRIST

GOD LOVES YOU

FACT:

FASTING STEERS THINGS IN THE RIGHT DIRECTION

INSPIRATION:

GOD IS YOUR FRIEND

Destiny Come Forth

June 7

PRAYER:

MAY YOU FIND THE PLANS THAT GOD HAS FOR YOU

MAY YOU PROSPER AND BE IN GOOD HEALTH

MAY YOU COACH OTHER PEOPLE

MAY YOU BE A GOOD EXAMPLE

MAY YOU STEP OUT

AMEN

DECREE:

YOU ARE A PART OF THE BIGGEST FAMILY

GOD'S FAMILY LOVES YOU

WE APPRECIATE YOU DOING YOUR PART

YOU HAVE GREAT IDEAS

YOU ALWAYS FOLLOW THROUGH

FAST:

FASTING FIXES YOUR FOCUS

GOD LOVES YOU

INSPIRATION:

Destiny Come Forth

June 8

PRAYER:

MAY YOU BE THANKFUL

MAY YOU BE HAPPY INSIDE

MAY YOU BRING JOY TO OTHERS

MAY YOU MAKE THIS DAY YOURS

MAY YOU LIGHT UP THE WORLD

AMEN

DECREE:

YOU ARE VALUABLE

YOU ARE LIKE A BIG WRAPPED UP GIFT

YOU HAVE FUN INSIDE

YOU ARE ANTICIPATED

YOU ARE NEEDED

FACT:

FASTING HEALS

INSPIRATION:

YOU CAN TRUST GOD

Destiny Come Forth

June 9

PRAYER:

MAY YOU GRASP YOUR WORTH

MAY YOU LET GOD DEFINE YOU

MAY YOU STAY FOCUSED ON THE TRUTH

MAY YOU SEND UP SOME LOVE

MAY YOU SEND OUT SOME LOVE

AMEN

DECREE:

YOU ARE A GREAT PERSON

YOU HAVE A GREAT FUTURE

GOD HAS SET UP GREAT THINGS FOR YOU TO DO

PREPARE TO SHINE

THIS IS YOUR TIME

AMEN

FACT:

FASTING STIRS UP LOVE

INSPIRATION:

GOD IS THE SAME

Destiny Come Forth

June 10

PRAYER:

MAY YOU HAVE FUN TODAY

MAY YOU ENJOY WHAT YOU HAVE

MAY YOU LIVE IN PEACE

MAY YOU HEAR GOD'S WORDS

MAY YOU ALWAYS DO YOUR BEST

AMEN

DECREE:

YOU ARE A DEDICATED SERVANT

YOU ARE A JOY TO THE WORLD

YOU ARE CALLED BY GOD

YOU SIT IN HEAVENLY PLACES

YOU ARE A GREAT LEADER

FACT:

FASTING CHANGES YOUR LIFE

INSPIRATION:

WHEN GOD IS YOUR SOURCE YOU WILL HAVE MORE JOY

Destiny Come Forth

June 11

PRAYER:

MAY YOU GAIN STRENGTH

MAY YOU USE GOD'S MOMENTUM

MAY YOU BREATHE IN GOD'S BEST

MAY YOU BE RECHARGED

MAY YOU LAST AND LAST

AMEN

DECREE:

YOU ARE A SOLID EXAMPLE

YOU ARE GROWING

YOU ARE ALWAYS ADVANCING

YOU TAKE TIME TO NOTICE THE PEOPLE IN FRONT OF YOU

YOU CARE ABOUT WHAT GOD CARES ABOUT

DECREE:

FASTING SETS THINGS IN MOTION

INSPIRATION:

SURROUND YOURSELF WITH LOVING PEOPLE

Destiny Come Forth

June 12

PRAYER:

MAY YOU SERVE GOD AND PEOPLE

MAY YOU GIVE ENDLESSLY

MAY YOU REACH UP TO GOD WITH LOVE

MAY YOU STAY FILLED UP

MAY YOU REACH OUT TO OTHERS WITH LOVE

AMEN

DECREE:

YOU ARE WISE

YOU BRING GIFTS TO THE LORD

YOU EXTEND YOURSELF

YOU DO MORE THAN YOU THOUGHT POSSIBLE

GOD IS YOUR ALLY

FACT:

FASTING FIXES THINGS

INSPIRATION:

MAKE AN IMPACT

Destiny Come Forth

June 13

PRAYER:

MAY YOU HEAR GOD

MAY YOU OBEY GOD

MAY YOU GIVE GOD YOUR ALL

MAY YOU REVERE GOD

MAY YOU REJOICE ALWAYS

AMEN

DECREE:

YOU ARE STRONGER THAN YOU THINK

YOU ARE WISER THAN YOU KNOW

YOU ARE GIFTED BY GOD

YOUR TALENTS INCREASE

YOU ARE GENEROUS

FACT:

FASTING TURNS ON A HOLY SIGNAL

INSPIRATION:

JESUS BROKE US ALL OUT OF THE BOX

Destiny Come Forth

June 14

PRAYER:

MAY YOU FEEL REFRESHED

MAY YOU REFRESH OTHERS

MAY YOU STEP OUT OF THE BOAT

MAY YOU WALK ON WATER

MAY YOU CHART A NEW PATH

AMEN

DECREE:

YOU ARE BRAVE

YOU ARE WILLING TO STRETCH YOURSELF

YOU ARE FUN TO WATCH

YOU MAKE THE IMPOSSIBLE REACHABLE

YOU ARE A TREND SETTER

FACT:

FASTING SEIZES OPPORTUNITY

INSPIRATION:

WE ARE ALL IN A PROCESS

Destiny Come Forth

June 15

PRAYER:

MAY YOU BE BLESSED

MAY YOU BLESS OTHERS

MAY YOUR LINEAGE BE BLESSED

MAY YOU LOVE YOUR LEGACY

MAY YOU LIVE IN THE MOMENT

AMEN

DECREE:

YOU ARE RIGHT ON TRACK

YOU PUSH THROUGH THE OBSTACLES

YOU KEEP MOVING NO MATTER WHAT

YOU HELP OTHER PEOPLE ALONG THE WAY

FACT:

FASTING TAKES PRACTICE

INSPIRATION:

LOVE IS BEAUTY FULL

Destiny Come Forth

June 16

PRAYER:

MAY YOU BE FILLED WITH JOY

MAY YOU SPREAD JOY TO OTHERS

MAY YOU BRING HEAVEN TO EARTH

MAY YOU BELIEVE IN YOURSELF

MAY YOU GET THINGS DONE

AMEN

DECREE:

YOU ARE A MASTERPIECE

YOU ARE MADE BY THE MASTER POTTER

YOU ARE FRESHLY ANOINTED

YOUR BLOODLINE IS CLEAN

YOU ARE GOOD

FACT:

FASTING CLEARS THE AIR

INSPIRATION:

GOD IS HELPING YOU

Destiny Come Forth

June 17

PRAYER:

MAY YOU CELEBRATE EVERY VICTORY

MAY YOU ENJOY YOUR REWARD

MAY YOU WALK WITH AUTHORITY

MAY YOU HAVE HOPE

MAY YOU TAKE HEART

AMEN

DECREE:

YOU ARE STRONG

YOU ARE GOING FURTHER THAN BEFORE

YOU EXPECT GOD TO SHOW UP

YOU TRUST IN GOD

GOD LOVES YOU

FACT:

FASTING OPENS DOORS

INSPIRATION:

FROM SHAME TO SHINE

Destiny Come Forth

June 18

PRAYER:

MAY YOU DIVE INTO GOD'S ARMS

MAY YOU BE SURROUNDED BY HIS LOVE

MAY YOU REACH FOR NEW THINGS

MAY YOUR FEET BE SECURE

MAY YOU BE SAFE

AMEN

DECREE:

YOU DO NOT PUT UP WITH DISHONESTY

YOU FOLLOW GOD

YOU BELIEVE FOR THE BEST

YOU REACH THE UNREACHABLE

YOU ARE A PIONEER

DECREE:

FASTING OPENS YOUR EYES

INSPIRATION:

YOU NEED DIFFERENT BAIT TO CATCH DIFFERENT FISH

Destiny Come Forth

June 19

PRAYER:

MAY YOU LOOK FOR OPPORTUNITIES TO SERVE

MAY YOU BOW DOWN LOW

MAY YOU GO FORWARD TODAY WITH HUMILITY

MAY YOU ACCEPT THE ADVANCEMENT OF GOD

MAY YOU DO YOUR BEST

AMEN

DECREE:

YOU ARE AMAZED AT THE GOODNESS OF GOD

FAVOR CHASES YOU

YOU CAN'T ESCAPE GOD'S LOVE

YOU CAN'T HELP BUT SHARE THE TRUTH

GOD LOVES US ALL

FACT:

FASTING SETS YOU APART

INSPIRATION:

DO THE RIGHT THINGS

Destiny Come Forth

June 20

PRAYER:

MAY YOU REFRESH OTHERS

MAY YOU BLESS OTHERS

MAY YOU TRUST OTHERS

MAY YOU BELIEVE FOR THE BEST

MAY YOU TRUST GOD WITH THE REST

AMEN

DECREE:

GOD IS WITH YOU

IT IS OBVIOUS

YOU ARE A BLESSING TO EVERYONE YOU MEET

YOU HAVE A HEART OF GOLD

YOU ARE SUGAR SWEET

FACT:

FASTING SERVES OTHERS

INSPIRATION:

WORK TOWARD UNITY

Destiny Come Forth

June 21

PRAYER:

MAY YOU DREAM BIG

MAY YOU ACHIEVE YOUR DREAMS

MAY YOU MOVE FORWARD WITH CONFIDENCE

MAY YOU BREAK THROUGH NEGATIVITY

MAY YOU BE FILLED WITH PEACE

AMEN

DECREE:

YOU ARE A LIGHT

YOU ARE LIKE A CITY ON A HILL

YOU BRING PEACE TO OTHERS

YOU ARE LOVED

YOU KNOW GOD PERSONALLY

FACT:

FASTING BRINGS LOVE

INSPIRATION:

BE MORE LIKE JESUS

Destiny Come Forth

June 22

PRAYER:

MAY YOU KEEP YOUR FOOTING

MAY YOU STAY STRONG IN THE LORD

MAY YOUR FAMILY AND FRIENDS LOVE YOU

MAY YOU FEEL THE LOVE

MAY YOU BE BLESSED

AMEN

DECREE:

YOU CAN FACE THE STORMS OF THIS LIFE

YOU LOOK GOOD IN THE WIND AND RAIN

YOUR LEGS ARE STRONG

YOU KNOW THAT LIFE IS SHORT

HEAVEN REJOICES OVER YOU

FACT:

FASTING DELIVERS

INSPIRATION:

HEAVEN IS REAL

Destiny Come Forth

June 23

PRAYER:

MAY YOU FOCUS ON WHAT REALLY MATTERS

MAY YOU HELP OTHER PEOPLE SEE GOD'S PLAN

MAY YOU INTERPRET THE BLUEPRINT

MAY YOU GLADLY DO YOUR PART

MAY YOU HELP OTHERS DO THEIR PART

AMEN

DECREE:

YOU ARE BRAVE

YOU LOOK INTO THE DAY WITH COURAGE

YOU HAVE THE STRENGTH TO BLAZE A NEW TRAIL

YOU HAVE WAITED LONG ENOUGH

IT'S YOUR TIME TO PIONEER

FACT:

FASTING STRENGTHENS YOUR BELIEF

INSPIRATION:

GOD WILL NEVER GIVE YOU BAD THOUGHTS

Destiny Come Forth

June 24

PRAYER:

MAY YOUR LIGHT NEVER DIM

MAY YOU GLOW WITH GOD

MAY THE GLORY OF GOD RUN THROUGH YOU

MAY YOU LOOK LIKE JESUS MORE AND MORE

MAY YOU DANCE THE DARKNESS AWAY

AMEN

DECREE:

YOU HAVE BEEN GIVEN AUTHORITY

YOU USE YOUR INFLUENCE TO HELP PEOPLE

YOU ARE AN INSTRUMENT IN THE HAND OF GOD

GOD USES YOU TO SHIFT THE ATMOSPHERE

FACT:

FASTING HELPS YOU FOCUS ON GOD

INSPIRATION:

LOVE PEOPLE

Destiny Come Forth

June 25

PRAYER:

MAY YOU DREAM OF GOD

MAY YOUR LIFE BE FILLED WITH GODLY PEOPLE

MAY YOU KNOW YOUR WORTH

MAY YOU DRAW CLOSER TO GOD

MAY YOU HELP OTHERS DRAW CLOSE

AMEN

DECREE:

YOU ARE A GREAT AND MIGHTY WARRIOR

YOU FIGHT TO WIN

YOUR FAITH IS STRONG

YOU KNOW THAT GOD IS WITH YOU

YOU BRING VICTORY TO EARTH

FACT:

FASTING BRINGS PEACE

INSPIRATION:

DON'T IGNORE THE HOLY SPIRIT

Destiny Come Forth

June 26

PRAYER:

MAY YOU JUMP FOR JOY

MAY YOU SHOUT HIS PRAISE

MAY YOU RELEASE HIS PRESENCE

MAY YOUR DAY BE BLESSED

MAY YOU KNOW YOUR POTENTIAL

AMEN

DECREE:

YOU ARE FULL OF JOY

YOU ARE FULL OF HOPE

YOU ARE FULL OF LOVE

YOU ARE FULL OF PEACE

YOU ARE WALKING IN VICTORY

FACT:

FASTING FUELS GOD'S COMPASSION IN YOU

INSPIRATION:

GOD CAN NOT BE CONTAINED

Destiny Come Forth

June 27

PRAYER:

MAY YOU GROW UPRIGHT

MAY YOU STAND TALL

MAY YOU FIND PEACE

MAY YOU SHOW LOVE

MAY YOU CARE DEEPLY

AMEN

DECREE:

YOU ARE MORE THAN A BELIEVER

YOU ARE STRONGER THAN YOU THINK

YOUR LIFE IS A LIGHT TO THE DARKNESS

YOU BRING HOPE TO THE HOPELESS

YOU ARE MADE NEW

FACT:

FASTING BRINGS FORTH VICTORY

INSPIRATION:

GET TO KNOW THE HOLY SPIRIT

Destiny Come Forth

June 28

PRAYER:

MAY YOU SEEK THE LORD FIRST

MAY YOU FOLLOW THE LORD

MAY YOU FIND WHAT YOU ARE LOOKING FOR

MAY YOU KEEP LOOKING FOR GOOD

MAY YOU MAKE GOD PROUD

AMEN

DECREE:

YOU STEP UP TO THE CHALLENGE

YOU GO FORWARD WITH GOD'S HELP

YOU KNOW THAT YOU CAN DO IT

YOU TRUST GOD COMPLETELY

YOU LOOK BACK ONLY TO LEARN

FACT:

FASTING STABILIZES YOUR LIFE

INSPIRATION:

GOD IS WITH US

Destiny Come Forth

June 29

PRAYER:

MAY YOU SEEK THE LORD FIRST

MAY YOU HELP OTHER PEOPLE MAKE GOD A PRIORITY

MAY YOU PRIORITIZE THE WORD OF GOD

MAY YOU INSTRUCT YOUR FAMILY AND FRIENDS

MAY YOU BE BRAVE TODAY

AMEN

DECREE:

YOU ARE SOLID

YOU ARE FULL OF THE POWER OF GOD

YOU MAKE A DIFFERENCE EVERYWHERE YOU GO

GOD ORDERS YOUR STEPS

YOU OBEY GOD SWIFTLY

FACT:

FAST EVERY WEEK

INSPIRATION:

STRETCH YOURSELF

Destiny Come Forth

June 30

PRAYER:

MAY YOU STAY RESILIENT

MAY GOD BE YOUR ANCHOR

MAY YOU STAY FOCUSED ON WHAT GOD IS DOING

MAY YOU GIVE GOD YOUR FULL ATTENTION

MAY YOU OBEY GOD'S EVERY COMMAND

AMEN

DECREE:

YOU ARE MORE THAN ENOUGH

THERE IS PLENTY TO GO AROUND

YOU GO AROUND DOING GOOD

YOU ARE AN ASSET TO GOD

YOU ENJOY YOUR BLESSINGS

FACT:

FASTING COMFORTS YOUR SPIRIT AND SOUL

INSPIRATION:

YOU HAVE TO START SOMEDAY SO START TODAY

Destiny Come Forth

July 1

PRAYER:

MAY YOU LIVE THE WAY YOU SHOULD

MAY YOU LEAD OTHERS INTO GOD'S PROMISES

MAY YOU SEEK GOD'S BEST TODAY

MAY YOU HONOR YOUR COUNTRY

MAY YOU BE OF SOME ASSISTANCE

AMEN

DECREE:

YOU ARE A JOY TO BE AROUND

YOU BRING COMFORT

GOD FLOWS THROUGH YOUR WORDS

HIS PRESENCE IS ALL AROUND YOU

YOU SHIFT THE ATMOSPHERE

FACT:

FASTING BRINGS PEACE

INSPIRATION:

BOOM AND BLOOM

Destiny Come Forth

July 2

PRAYER:

MAY YOU ENJOY YOUR DAY

MAY YOU FEEL SPECIAL

MAY YOU HELP OTHERS FEEL SPECIAL

MAY YOU RECOGNIZE YOUR UNIQUE GIFT

MAY YOU IGNITE HEARTS FOR THE KINGDOM

AMEN

DECREE:

YOU ARE UNIQUE

YOU ARE BLESSED AND HIGHLY FAVORED

YOU CAN DO IT

YOU HAVE BEEN ORDAINED BY GOD

GOD WANTS TO SEE YOU THRIVE

FACT:

FASTING GROWS YOUR TESTIMONY

INSPIRATION:

GOD SAID IT IS GOOD

Destiny Come Forth

July 3

PRAYER:

MAY YOU RISE UP AND SHOUT GOD'S PRAISE TODAY

MAY YOU TAKE TO HEART GOD'S GOOD NEWS

MAY YOU CELEBRATE WITH ALL YOUR STRENGTH THIS DAY

MAY YOU RECEIVE GOD'S BLESSINGS FOR YOU

MAY YOU ENJOY THIS TIME IN LIFE TO THE FULLEST

AMEN

DECREE:

YOU ARE STRONGER THAN YOU THINK

YOU THINK BIGGER

GOD IS KINDER THAN YOU KNOW

GOD IS HAPPY WITH YOU

YOU ARE GOD'S BELOVED CHILD

FACT:

FASTING EMPOWERS YOU

INSPIRATION:

GOD KEEPS NO RECORD OF WRONG

Destiny Come Forth

July 4

PRAYER:

MAY YOU ALWAYS ENJOY WHAT YOU HAVE

MAY YOU SHARE WHAT YOU HAVE

MAY GOD MULTIPLY WHAT YOU HAVE

MAY YOUR LIFE MAGNIFY WHAT GOD IS DOING

MAY YOU REJOICE WITH ALL OF HEAVEN TODAY

AMEN

DECREE:

YOU ARE SATISFIED

YOU EXPECT MORE FOR OTHERS

YOU CONTEND FOR GOD'S FAMILY INHERITANCE

YOUR PRAYERS ARE POWERFUL

YOU ARE PART OF THE BIG PICTURE

FACT:

FASTING BRINGS REVIVAL

INSPIRATION:

REMIND GOD OF HIS PROMISES

Destiny Come Forth

July 5

PRAYER:

MAY YOU LOOK TO GOD TODAY FOR THE ANSWERS

MAY YOU ONLY BELIEVE GOD'S REPORT

MAY YOU CLING TO THE TRUTH OF THE GOOD NEWS

MAY YOU REPORT TRIUMPH AFTER TRIUMPH

MAY YOU STAY ABOVE BOARD

AMEN

DECREE:

YOU ARE MIGHTY IN GOD

YOU SHINE RIGHT THROUGH EVERYTHING

YOU ARE SOMEONE TO BE ADMIRED

GOD IS VERY GLAD TO KNOW YOU

YOU HURDLE OVER EVERY OBSTACLE

FACT:

FASTING REVEALS THE PLANS OF GOD

INSPIRATION:

YOU WILL KNOW CHRISTIANS BY THEIR LOVE

Destiny Come Forth

July 6

PRAYER:

MAY YOU DAY BE FULL OF GUMPTION

MAY YOU FIND WHAT YOU ARE LOOKING FOR

MAY YOU SEE THINGS YOU HAVE NEVER SEEN BEFORE

MAY YOU HELP OTHERS KNOW THE TRUTH

MAY YOU ENJOY YOUR VICTORIES

AMEN

DECREE:

YOU HAVE BECOME DELIBERATE

YOU CHOOSE WELL

YOU ARE DETERMINED TO DO GREAT THINGS FOR THE FAMILY OF GOD

GOD HELPS YOU AND YOUR FAMILY

YOUR VICTORY IS SECURE

FACT:

FASTING GROWS TRUST

INSPIRATION:

JESUS IS YOUR HERO

Destiny Come Forth

July 7

PRAYER:

MAY YOUR DAY REACH NEW HEIGHTS

MAY YOU LOVE YOUR LIFE

MAY YOU HELP OTHERS LOVE THEIR LIFE

MAY YOU FOCUS ON THE GOOD THINGS THAT ARE HAPPENING

MAY YOU BE A PART OF THE GOOD

AMEN

DECREE:

GOD HELPS YOU SET YOUR GOALS

YOU ACCOMPLISH EVERYTHING WITH GOD'S HELP

NOTHING IS TOO HARD FOR YOU

YOU WERE CREATED TO RISE AND SHINE ABOVE IT ALL

YOU ARE A FRIEND OF GOD'S

FACT:

FASTING RELIEVES STRESS

INSPIRATION:

GOD'S WORD IS WORTH MORE THAN IT'S WEIGHT IN GOLD

Destiny Come Forth

July 8

PRAYER:

MAY YOU HONOR GOD TODAY

MAY YOU HELP OTHERS GIVE GLORY TO GOD

MAY YOU BE OPEN TO CHANGE

MAY YOUR EYES BE OPENED TOWARD GOD

MAY YOU SEE THE PLAN

AMEN

DECREE:

YOU HAVE A GREAT GOD ON YOUR SIDE

HOLY JUSTICE IS COMING

FREEDOM IS YOURS

YOU LOVE WITH LUSH LIBERTY

HEAVEN PROTECTS YOU AND YOURS

FACT:

FASTING SURROUNDS YOU WITH HOLY PROTECTION

INSPIRATION:

PLANT YOUR FEET ON HOLY GROUND

Destiny Come Forth

July 9

PRAYER:

MAY YOUR DAY START OUT RIGHT

MAY YOU MOTIVATE OTHERS

MAY YOU GO TO GOD AND SET YOUR GOALS

MAY YOU TRUST COMPLETELY IN GOD

MAY YOU LIVE VICTORIOUSLY

AMEN

DECREE:

YOU TRY AND TRY AGAIN

YOU ARE DETERMINED TO WIN

GOD HAS GREAT PLANS FOR YOU

YOU HAVE BEEN CHOSEN

YOU DO THE RIGHT THINGS

FACT:

FASTING BRINGS IMMENSE FAVOR

INSPIRATION:

GREAT WILL BE YOUR REWARD

Destiny Come Forth

July 10

PRAYER:

MAY YOU RUSH FORWARD WITH AUTHORITY

MAY YOU BRING HEAVEN TO EARTH

MAY YOU KNOW YOUR POWER IN CHRIST

MAY YOU BELIEVE YOU CAN DO IT

MAY YOU FULFILL YOUR DESTINY

AMEN

DECREE:

YOU PRESS THROUGH

YOU HURDLE EVERY HUMP

YOU MOVE FORWARD WITH GOD'S SUPERNATURAL POWER

NOTHING CAN STOP YOU

YOU ARE A WINNER

FACT:

FASTING HELPS YOU WIN

INSPIRATION:

GOD WILL GIVE YOU EVERYTHING YOU NEED

Destiny Come Forth

July 11

PRAYER:

MAY YOU KNOW YOU ARE MORE THAN ENOUGH

MAY YOU GIVE MORE THAN YOU TAKE

MAY YOU DO GREAT THINGS

MAY YOU BE AN ASSET TO GOD

MAY YOU ENJOY YOUR BLESSINGS

AMEN

DECREE:

GOD LOVES YOU

JESUS SAVED YOU

THE HOLY SPIRIT EMPOWERS YOU

HOLY ANGELS SURROUND YOU

YOU SHAKE THE EARTH WITH YOUR TESTIMONY

FACT:

FASTING MAKES YOU STRONG AND COURAGEOUS

INSPIRATION:

THE HOLY SPIRIT CANNOT BE CONTAINED

Destiny Come Forth

July 12

PRAAYER:

MAY YOU BELIEVE IN YOURSELF

MAY YOU STAND UP STRAIGHT

MAY YOU WALK THE NARROW PATH

MAY YOU STAY ON TRACK

MAY YOU MAKE IT TO HEAVEN

AMEN

DECREE:

YOU HAVE CREDIBLE VALUE

YOU ARE WORTH MORE THAN YOU KNOW

YOUR HOLY INTENSITY IS GROWING

YOU ARE IN PLACE TO PROSPER AND WALK IN DIVINE HEALTH

YOUR CHOICES BLESS OTHERS

FACT:

FASTING OPENS HEAVEN'S GATES

INSPIRATION:

GOD FLOATS YOUR BOAT

Destiny Come Forth

July 13

PRAYER:

MAY YOUR BURDEN BE LIFTED

MAY YOUR YOKE BE EASY

MAY YOU BE PAIRED UP EQUALLY

MAY YOU BE FAVORED

MAY YOUR DAY GO JUST AS GOD PLANNED

DECREE:

YOU ARE A GOOD STEWARD

YOU ARE ALWAYS THERE FOR YOUR LOVED ONES

YOUR OWN NEEDS ARE MET

YOUR PRAYERS ARE HEARD AND ANSWERED

YOU PRAY IN AGREEMENT WITH GOD

FACT:

FASTING IS FUN

INSPIRATION:

THINK POSITIVE ABOUT EVERYTHING

Destiny Come Forth

July 14

PRAYER:

MAY YOU BREAK THROUGH

MAY YOU LIGHT UP THE DARKNESS

MAY YOU BRING HOPE TO ALL

MAY YOU OPEN YOUR EYES TO SEE GOD'S GLORY

MAY YOU WIN WITH A GRIN

DECREE:

YOU ARE OUT IN FRONT

YOU ARE AHEAD

YOU ARE ABOVE

YOU ARE ALWAYS IN A GREAT PLACE WITH GOD

YOU HAVE A SOLID POSITION

FACT:

FASTING BRINGS NEW OPPORTUNITIES

INSPIRATION:

USE YOUR SWORD

JESUS CHRIST IS LORD

Destiny Come Forth

July 15

PRAYER:

MAY YOU FEEL SOLID

MAY YOUR FEET BE SECURE

MAY YOUR STRENGTH BE RENEWED

MAY YOUR STEPS BE ORDERED BY GOD

MAY YOU OBEY HIS CALLING

AMEN

DECREE:

YOU PONDER DEEP REVELATION

YOU KNOW THE TIMES AND THE SEASONS

YOU ARE GOD'S HOLY DELEGATE

GOD IS DELIGHTED TO CALL YOU HIS CHILD

YOU ARE WELL KNOWN AND LOVED

FACT:

FASTING FINDS A WAY

INSPIRATION:

REMEMBER THAT GOD HAS THE FINAL SAY

Destiny Come Forth

July 16

PRAYER:

MAY YOU STRETCH YOURSELF

MAY YOU REACH OUT OF THE BOX

MAY YOU BRING OTHERS OUT OF THE BOX TOO

MAY YOUR THINKING BE WISE

MAY YOU WALK WITH YOUR GOD-GIVEN AUTHORITY

AMEN

DECREE:

YOU ARE SOPHISTICATED

YOU HAVE BEEN SEASONED WITH GOD'S LOVE

YOU ARE THE SALT OF THE EARTH

YOU SEEK GOD'S TRUTH

YOU ARE SANCTIFIED

FACT:

FASTING BRINGS WISDOM

INSPIRATION:

GOD WILL BRING YOU TO YOUR CALLING IF YOU FOLLOW HIM

Destiny Come Forth

July 17

PRAYER:

MAY YOU SEEK GOD FOR YOUR LIFE

MAY YOU SEEK GOD FOR YOUR FAMILY AND FRIENDS

MAY YOU SEEK GOD FOR YOUR COMMUNITY

MAY YOU SEEK GOD FOR YOUR COUNTRY

MAY YOU SEEK TO PLEASE GOD

AMEN

DECREE:

YOU LIVE IT UP

YOU GIVE IT ALL UP TO GOD

YOU TRUST GOD WITH THE RESULTS

YOU STAY FOCUSSED ON YOUR GOALS SET BY GOD

YOU TRY HARD BY DOING YOUR PART

FACT:

FASTING TEACHES YOU SELF-CONTROL

INSPIRATION:

FOLLOW GOD INTO VICTORY

Destiny Come Forth

July 18

PRAYER:

MAY YOU WATCH GOD

MAY YOU HEAR GOD

MAY YOU TOUCH GOD

MAY YOU SHARE THE LOVE OF GOD

MAY YOU INVEST IN THE THINGS OF GOD

AMEN

DECREE:

YOU MAKE WISE CHOICES

YOU HELP OTHER PEOPLE LEARN

YOU SHARE YOUR FAITH

YOU BELIEVE FOR THE IMPOSSIBLE

GOD ANSWERS YOUR PRAYERS

FACT:

FASTING PURIFIES YOUR THOUGHTS

INSPIRATION:

FIX YOUR EYES ON WHAT GOD HAS FIXED

Destiny Come Forth

July 19

PRAYER:

MAY YOU BELIEVE WHAT GOD SAYS ABOUT YOU

MAY YOU WALK IN YOUR ANOINTING

MAY YOU BE CONFIDENT IN YOUR CALLING

MAY YOU FOLLOW THROUGH

MAY YOU BE INTENTIONAL

AMEN

DECREE:

YOU ARE INTELLIGENT

YOU ARE GENEROUS

YOU ARE A LOVE CHAMPION

YOU ARE SINCERE

YOU HONOR GOD

FACT:

FASTING MAKES YOU MORE LIKE JESUS

INSPIRATION:

ALWAYS TRY TO DO GOOD

Destiny Come Forth

July 20

PRAYER:

MAY YOUR LIFE BE A REFLECTION OF HEAVEN

MAY YOU FEEL LOVED

MAY YOU BE HONORED BY YOUR FAMILY

MAY GOD BLESS YOUR LIFE

MAY YOU BE CHERISHED

AMEN

DECREE:

YOU ARE LINED UP WITH GOD'S WORD

YOU ARE PREPARED TO SHINE FORWARD

YOU MAKE A WAY

YOU TAKE CHARGE

GOD IS WITH YOU EVERY STEP OF THE WAY

FACT:

FASTING IS COURAGEOUS

INSPIRATION:

ENJOY EVERY MOMENT

Destiny Come Forth

July 21

PRAYER:

MAY YOU KNOW WHAT GOD SAYS ABOUT YOU

MAY YOU UNDERSTAND IT

MAY YOU BELIEVE IT

MAY YOUR TIMING BE ALIGNED WITH GOD

MAY YOUR STEPS BE ORDERED

AMEN

DECREE:

YOU HONOR GOD

YOU HELP PEOPLE

YOU KEEP THE PLANS AND PURPOSES OF GOD IN CLEAR SIGHT

YOU WERE CREATED TO ACCOMPLISH GOD THINGS

YOU TAKE TIME TO REST

FACT:

FASTING IMPACTS GENERATIONS

INSPIRATION:

NEVER FORGET WHERE GOD HAS BROUGHT YOU FROM

Destiny Come Forth

July 22

PRAYER:

MAY YOU BE UNITED

MAY YOU CLEAR YOUR MIND

MAY YOU SEE CLEARLY

MAY YOU SURROUND YOURSELF WITH THE HOLY SPIRIT

MAY YOUR TIME BE SPENT WELL

AMEN

DECREE:

YOU ARE BLESSED BY GOD ALMIGHTY

GOD GUARDS YOU AND YOURS

YOU HAVE NOTHING TO FEAR

YOUR LIFE MESSAGE CHANGES LIVES

YOU BROADCAST HOPE

FACT:

FASTING SPEAKS LIFE

INSPIRATION:

GOD WILL NEVER ABANDON YOU

Destiny Come Forth

July 23

PRAYER:

MAY YOU BE FILLED WITH GOD'S PRESENCE

MAY GOD FLOW FROM YOU

MAY YOUR DAY BE PLEASANT

MAY THINGS GO GOD'S WAY

MAY YOU BE FILLED WITH HOPE

AMEN

DECREE:

YOU TAKE CARE OF YOURSELF

YOU HELP OTHERS WITH YOUR INNER STRENGTH

YOU ARE ON GOD'S TEAM

YOU DO EVERYTHING UNTO THE LORD

GOD IS WELL PLEASED WITH YOU

FACT:

FASTING KEEPS YOUR MIND ON GOD

INSPIRATION:

THE FRAGRANCE OF GOD IS PLEASANT

Destiny Come Forth

July 24

PRAYER:

MAY YOU BE JOY FULL

MAY YOU FIND THE GOOD IN THIS WORLD

MAY YOU MAGNIFY IT

MAY YOU SPEAK LIFE

MAY YOUR OUTLOOK BE POSITIVE

AMEN

DECREE:

YOU ARE ON TRACK AND MOVING FORWARD

YOU ARE BELIEVING FOR THE BEST

YOU ACHIEVE VICTORY IN ALL YOU DO

YOU WERE CREATED TO EXCEL

YOU GIVE ENDLESSLY

FACT:

FASTING BRINGS REWARDS FROM GOD

INSPIRATION:

SURROUND YOURSELF WITH GOD'S PEOPLE

Destiny Come Forth

July 25

PRAYER:

MAY YOUR LIFE BE PEACEFUL

MAY YOU HAVE PATIENCE

MAY YOU KNOW WHAT TO SAY

MAY YOU KNOW WHEN TO SAY IT

MAY YOU CHANGE LIVES

AMEN

DECREE:

YOU MARCH FORWARD

YOU OBEY GOD SWIFTLY

YOUR FAITH HAS BEEN INCREASED

YOU CAN SEE THE POTENTIAL IN OTHERS

YOU ARE A PRIME EXAMPLE

FACT:

FASTING MAKES YOU BOLD

INSPIRATION:

BE FULL OF COMPASSION

Destiny Come Forth

July 26

PRAYER:

MAY YOU BE SOLID IN YOUR FAITH

MAY YOU SHARE YOUR FAITH WITH OTHERS

MAY YOU SHINE WITH GOD'S LOVE

MAY YOU RESPECT GOD

MAY YOU BE RESPECTED

AMEN

DECREE:

GOD IS ALWAYS WITH YOU

YOU HAVE MORE HELP THAN YOU KNOW

HEAVEN REJOICES WITH YOU

YOU ARE A PIONEER

YOU MAKE A JOYFUL WAY FOR OTHERS

FACT:

FASTING REVIVES HOPE

INSPIRATION:

THE HOLY SPIRIT LIKES TO CHALLENGE YOU

Destiny Come Forth

July 27

PRAYER:

MAY YOU FIND GOD OUT IN FRONT OF YOU

MAY YOU FOLLOW CLOSELY

MAY YOU STAY ON YOUR LIFE PATH

MAY YOU STAY CONTENT WITH YOUR WALK

MAY YOU WALK WITH JOY

AMEN

DECREE:

YOU ARE BLESSED BY GOD

YOUR WHOLE FAMILY IS BLESSED

YOU TOUCH THE UNIVERSE WITH YOUR STRENGTH

YOU SHAKE AND SETTLE THINGS

YOU ARE OPPORTUNE

FACT:

FASTING SAVES YOU MONEY

INSPIRATION:

YOU ARE A GIFT

Destiny Come Forth

July 28

PRAYER:

MAY YOU TAKE TIME TO REFRESH YOURSELF

MAY YOU LEAN INTO GOD

MAY YOU GAIN STRENGTH

MAY YOU TAKE BACK TIME

MAY YOU TRUST GOD FULLY

AMEN

DECREE:

YOU ARE MORE THAN ENOUGH

YOUR CUP OVERFLOWS

GOD KEEPS POURING MORE INTO YOU

YOU SHARE FROM YOUR OVERLOAD

IT'S A PLEASURE KNOWING YOU

FACT:

FASTING CUTS THROUGH

INSPIRATION:

MOVE WITH GOD

Destiny Come Forth

July 29

PRAYER:

MAY YOU BE CONSIDERATE TODAY

MAY YOU BE JOYFUL

MAY HAPPINESS BE FOUND IN YOU

MAY GOOD TIMES BE NEAR

MAY YOU BE SURROUNDED BY POSSIBILITY

AMEN

DECREE:

YOU ARE BOLDER THAN ANY BOULDER

YOU ARE CRYING OUT FOR VICTORY

YOU BELIEVE THE BEST IS YET TO COME

YOU HELP OTHERS SEEK GOD'S BEST

YOU ARE CONFIDENT

FACT:

FASTING DRIVES YOU FORWARD

INSPIRATION:

RISE UP IN THE POWER OF GOD'S LOVE

Destiny Come Forth

July 30

PRAYER:

MAY YOU FOLLOW THROUGH

MAY YOU BE DETERMINED

MAY YOU FEEL LOVED AND CONFIDENT

MAY YOU BE PREPARED FOR GOD'S BLESSING

MAY YOU DO GOD'S WILL

AMEN

DECREE:

YOU PUT YOUR BEST FEET FORWARD

YOU RISE UP AND SHINE

YOU UNDERSTAND OTHERS

YOU LOVE THEM WITH COMPASSION

YOU SHARE YOUR GIFTS AND TALENTS

FACT:

FASTING MULTIPLIES YOUR BLESSINGS

INSPIRATION:

PRAY OFTEN

Destiny Come Forth

July 31

PRAYER:

MAY YOU LOOK AROUND TO SEE THE TRUTH

MAY YOU COME TO TERMS WITH LIFE

MAY YOU ENJOY THE PRESENT MOMENT

MAT YOU FOCUS ON GOD

MAY YOU BECOME MORE LIKE HIM

AMEN

DECREE:

YOU ARE A CONQUEROR

YOU ARE A TOOL IN THE HAND OF GOD

YOU HAVE BEEN MADE WITH PRECISION

GOD USES YOU TO TIGHTEN THINGS UP

YOU WORK WELL

FACT:

FASTING BREAKS FOOD ADDICTION

INSPIRATION:

BE AN ACTIVE PART OF THE FAMILY OF GOD

Destiny Come Forth

August 1

PRAYER:

MAY GOD BE THE ANCHOR OF YOUR SOUL

MAY YOU SOAR HIGH

MAY YOU TAKE CARE OF YOUR BODY

MAY YOU ENCOURAGE PEOPLE TO THRIVE

MAY YOU BE THANKFUL

AMEN

DECREE:

YOU ARE FULL OF GOD'S PROMISES

YOU KNOW THAT GOD IS GOOD

YOU TRUST IN THE TRUTH

YOU ARE STRONG AND READY

YOU TAKE A BOLD HOLD OF GOD'S WORD

FACT:

FASTING ENTRUSTS EVERYTHING TO GOD

INSPIRATION:

GOD IS WELL PLEASED WITH YOU

Destiny Come Forth

August 2

PRAYER:

MAY YOU ALWAYS BE READY TO GO

MAY YOU HAVE AN OBEDIENT HEART

MAY YOU BE WILLING

MAY YOU HAVE A VISION FOR A BETTER WORLD

MAY YOU BE A PART OF THE RESOLVE

AMEN

DECREE:

YOU LOVE

YOU CARE

YOU BRING PEACE

YOU LIGHT UP THIS WORLD

YOU CHANGE THINGS

FACT:

FASTING FILLS YOU WITH FAITH

INSPIRATION:

GOD IS YOUR HOLY HERO

Destiny Come Forth

August 3

PRAYER:

MAY YOU STAY ON TRACK

MAY YOU LOVE TO BE WITH GOD

MAY YOU BE AN INSTRUMENT OF GOD'S PEACE

MAY YOU BE THE APPLE OF GOD'S EYE

MAY YOU BE BLESSED AND BLESS OTHERS

AMEN

DECREE:

YOU GO STRAIGHT FOR THE VICTORY

YOU DON'T DELAY

YOU HAVE HOLY ZEAL

YOU FOLLOW THROUGH

YOU FINISH WHAT GOD ASKS YOU TO DO

FACT:

FASTING HELPS YOU STAY ON TOP OF THINGS

INSPIRATION:

GOD BELIEVES IN YOU

Destiny Come Forth

August 4

PRAYER:

MAY YOU DO THE RIGHT THINGS

MAY GOD'S LIGHT SHINE THROUGH YOU

MAY YOU BE FUN TO BE AROUND

MAY YOU BRING JOY EVERYWHERE YOU GO

MAY YOU MAKE LIFE BETTER

AMEN

DECREE:

YOU ARE HANDY

YOU ARE HERE TO HELP

YOU MAKE POSITIVE CHANGES

YOU ARE SETTING THE PACE

YOU OVERCOME EVERY OBSTACLE

FACT:

FASTING HELPS YOU WIN THE RACE

INSPIRATION:

NEVER STOP PURSUING THE FATHER

Destiny Come Forth

August 5

PRAYER:

MAY YOUR INTENTIONS BE GOOD

MAY YOU DO YOUR BEST

MAY YOU HONOR GOD

MAY YOU TAKE CARE OF YOURSELF

MAY YOU TAKE CARE OF OTHERS

AMEN

DECREE:

YOU APPROACH EVERYTHING WITH LOVE

YOU BELIEVE FOR THE BEST

YOU REST BY GOD

YOU IGNITE COMPASSION

YOU DARE TO TRY NEW THINGS

FACT:

FASTING SETS THE TONE FOR YOUR DAY

INSPIRATION:

JESUS IS THE PRIME EXAMPLE OF LOVE

August 6

PRAYER:

MAY YOU FEEL SURROUNDED BY GOD'S LOVE

MAY YOU LOVE ALL PEOPLE

MAY YOU OFFER GRACE

MAY YOU LIVE IN PEACE

MAY YOU GRASP LIFE AND MAKE IT BETTER

AMEN

DECREE:

YOU ARE RIGHT ON

YOU HELP OTHERS FIND HOPE

YOU ACHIEVE YOUR TOP GOALS

YOU ARE SURPRISINGLY ENTHUSIASTIC

YOU ARE COMPASSIONATE

FACT:

FASTING PROTECTS YOU

INSPIRATION:

GOD APPRECIATES ALL THAT YOU DO

Destiny Come Forth

August 7

PRAYER:

MAY YOU BE SPONTANEOUS

MAY YOU BE THE "LIFE" OF THE PARTY

MAY YOUR SMILE EXPRESS GOD'S LOVE

MAY YOU HAVE HOLY HOPE

MAY YOU BE FREE

AMEN

DECREE:

YOU ARE FULLY ALIVE

YOU ARE DOING WELL

YOU BROADCAST THE GOOD NEWS

YOU SPREAD THE HOPE OF THE GOSPEL

YOU ARE A SOURCE OF JOY

FACT:

FASTING BRINGS FREEDOM

INSPIRATION:

INSTIGATE HOLY GROWTH

Destiny Come Forth

August 8

PRAYER:

MAY YOU BE FREE

MAY YOU VALUE YOUR INDEPENDENCE

MAY YOU BE GRATEFUL

MAY YOU HONOR OTHERS

MAY YOU DECREE JUSTICE

AMEN

DECREE:

YOU MARCH FORWARD

YOU LEAD MANY TO VICTORY

YOU ARE STRONG AND CHOSEN

YOU ARE COURAGEOUS

YOUR REWARD IS GREAT

FACT:

FASTING MAKES THE ENEMY TREMBLE

INSPIRATION:

NO WEAPON FORMED AGAINST YOU WILL PROSPER

Destiny Come Forth

August 9

PRAYER:

MAY YOU WALK IN TOTAL FORGIVENESS

MAY YOU COMPLETELY FORGIVE EVERYONE

MAY YOU BE KIND

MAY YOU BE FULL OF LOVE

MAY YOU BE THANK FULL

AMEN

DECREE:

YOU ARE ON A ROLL

YOUR ENERGY HAS MULTIPLIED

PEOPLE UNDERSTAND YOU

EVERYTHING HAS BEEN FORGIVEN

GOD'S LOVE COVERS ALL

FACT:

FASTING EXTINGUISHES NEGATIVITY

INSPIRATION:

GOD ANSWERS PRAYERS

Destiny Come Forth

August 10

PRAYER:

MAY YOU FIND VICTORY WITH EVERY STEP

MAY YOU SHARE YOUR EXCITEMENT

MAY YOU GIVE GOD THE CREDIT

MAY YOU EXPAND IN EVERY DIRECTION

MAY YOU USE YOUR GOD GIVEN AUTHORITY WELL

AMEN

DECREE:

YOU ALWAYS WIN

YOU HAVE LEARNED HOW TO WAIT FOR IT

GOD DEFENDS YOU

GOD TURNS EVERYTHING TO GOOD FOR YOU

YOU HELP A LOT OF PEOPLE

FACT:

FASTING HELPS

INSPIRATION:

BE TRUE

Destiny Come Forth

August 11

PRAYER:

MAY YOU BE RESTORED

MAY EVERYTHING BE RETURNED TO YOU

MAY YOU EXCEL

MAY GOD CONTINUE TO PREPARE YOU

MAY YOU KNOW YOUR WORTH

AMEN

DECREE:

YOU ARE MOTIVATED

YOU ARE ENCOURAGED

YOU ARE HEALTHY

YOU ARE CONTENT

YOU ACHIEVE GOD'S BEST

FACT:

FASTING MAKES YOU JOYFUL

INSPIRATION:

FOLLOW IN GOD'S FOOTSTEPS

Destiny Come Forth

August 12

PRAYER:

MAY YOU GO FOR IT

MAY YOU HELP OTHERS GO FOR IT

MAY YOU SET YOUR GOALS HIGH

MAY YOU LISTEN TO GOD

MAY YOU BELIEVE

AMEN

DECREE:

YOU ARE MADE IN THE IMAGE OF GOD

YOU ARE FEARLESS

YOU ARE STRONG

YOU BUILD BRIDGES

YOU DO ALL THINGS WELL

FACT:

FASTING REAPS REWARDS

INSPIRATION:

GOD'S TIMING IS NEVER WRONG

Destiny Come Forth

August 13

PRAYER:

MAY YOU HIT YOUR MARK

MAY YOU BE LIKE AN ARROW IN THE QUIVER OF GOD

MAY YOU BE SHARP

MAY YOU BE READY

MAY YOU HIT THE CENTER

AMEN

DECREE:

YOU LOVE TO LEARN

YOU TEACH OTHERS

YOU ARE FREE FROM SIN

YOU ARE FORGIVEN

YOU TRY HARD TO HELP OTHERS BE FREE

FACT:

FASTING IS A POWERFUL TOOL

INSPIRATION:

MARCH IN THE ARMY OF GOD

Destiny Come Forth

August 14

PRAYER:

MAY YOU BE AN ENCOURAGER

MAY YOU BE STEADFAST

MAY YOU ACCOMPLISH WHAT GOD GOD ASKS

MAY YOU BE FRIENDLY

MAY YOU WALK WITH GREAT FAVOR

AMEN

DECREE:

YOU ARE SPECIAL

YOU ARE SIGNIFICANT

YOU ARE TRUSTWORTHY

YOU ARE MATURE

YOU EXPECT HOLY ADVANCEMENT

FACT:

FASTING BRINGS GOD'S FAVOR

INSPIRATION:

SHARE YOUR INSIGHT

Destiny Come Forth

August 15

PRAYER:

MAY YOU HONOR GOD OUR FATHER

MAY YOU KNOW YOU ARE THE APPLE OF GOD'S EYE

MAY YOU KNOW GOD LOVES YOU IMMENSELY

MAY YOU BE KIND

MAY YOU ENCOURAGE OTHERS WITH THE SAME LOVE

AMEN

DECREE:

YOU ARE SURPRISINGLY WITTY

YOU ARE FUN TO BE WITH

YOU BRING THE JOY OF GOD

YOU ARE ESTEEMED

GOD IS HAPPY WITH YOU

FACT:

FASTING INITIATES THINGS IN THE SPIRITUAL REALM

INSPIRATION:

BRING HEAVEN TO US

Destiny Come Forth

August 16

PRAYER:

MAY YOU REACH UP TO GOD'S HEART

MAY YOU BRING DOWN HIS LOVE

MAY YOU PLANT LOVING SEEDS EVERYWHERE

MAY THEY GROW BIG AND TALL

MAY YOU REAP LOVE

AMEN

DECREE:

YOU GIVE YOUR FAMILY AND FRIENDS TIME

YOU ARE PATIENT

YOU ARE KIND AND LOVING

YOU ARE A GOOD EXAMPLE

YOU KEEP ENCOURAGING YOUR LOVED ONES

FACT:

FASTING STRENGTHENS HOPE

INSPIRATION:

GOD GIVES MORE THAN ENOUGH

Destiny Come Forth

August 17

PRAYER:

MAY YOU LOVE GOD WITH EVERYTHING THAT YOU HAVE

MAY YOU SHOW OTHERS HOW TO LOVE

MAY YOU PIONEER A LOVE TRAIL

MAY YOU KNOW HOW MUCH GOD LOVES YOU

MAY YOU BE RESPECTED BY YOUR PEERS

AMEN

DECREE:

YOU ARE AN AMAZING PART OF GOD'S CREATION

GOD CREATED YOU WITH A SPECIFIC PURPOSE

YOU HAVE FOUND YOUR DESTINY

YOU STAY ON TRACK

YOUR LEGACY IS BRIGHT

FACT:

FASTING STILLS THE FLESH

INSPIRATION:

USE WISDOM

Destiny Come Forth

August 18

PRAYER:

MAY YOU RISE UP

MAY YOU STAND TALL

MAY YOU SHINE BRIGHT

MAY YOU LOVE ALL

MAY YOU TESTIFY

AMEN

DECREE:

YOU ARE SAVED

YOU ARE SAFE

YOUR WHOLE HOUSEHOLD IS BLESSED

YOU ARE ANOINTED

YOU ARE SACRED

FACT:

FASTING FULFILLS GOD'S PEOPLE

INSPIRATION:

YOU ARE STRONG IN THE LORD

Destiny Come Forth

August 19

PRAYER:

MAY YOU KNOW WHERE YOUR HELP COMES FROM

MAY YOU WALK AND TALK LIKE JESUS

MAY YOU USE YOUR FULL AUTHORITY

MAY YOU FORGIVE EVERYONE

MAY YOU BE FREE INDEED

AMEN

DECREE:

YOU ARE KIND

YOU ARE GENTLE

YOU ARE SWEET

YOU ARE FUN

YOU ARE GENUINE

FACT:

FASTING IS SINCERE BEFORE GOD

INSPIRATION:

LET YOUR TRUE COLORS SHINE THROUGH

August 20

PRAYER:

MAY YOU LOVE GOD

MAY YOU LOVE PEOPLE

MAY YOU LOVE YOUR LIFE

MAY YOU ENCOURAGE OTHERS TO LOVE

MAY YOU ALWAYS TRY TO DO GREAT THINGS

AMEN

DECREE:

YOU ARE FREE

YOU LIBERATE OTHERS

YOU COUNT YOUR BLESSINGS

YOU STAY POSITIVE

YOU SEEK COUNSEL FROM GOD

FACT:

FASTING HELPS GOD SPEAK TO YOU

INSPIRATION:

HEAR OTHERS AND YOU WILL BE HEARD

Destiny Come Forth

August 21

PRAYER:

MAY YOU BE PUT ON THE TOP

MAY YOU SOAR ABOVE

MAY YOU CLIMB EVEN HIGHER

MAY YOU SEEK GOD

MAY GOD SEEK YOU

AMEN

DECREE:

YOU ARE OPEN

YOU ARE FLEXIBLE

YOU ARE LOVING

YOU ARE WILLING TO CHANGE

YOU ARE A TEAM PLAYER

FACT:

FASTING UNITES

INSPIRATION:

BE A BLESSING TO YOUR COMMUNITY

Destiny Come Forth

August 22

PRAYER:

MAY YOU BE OBEDIENT TO GOD

MAY YOU SERVE GOD WITH YOUR WHOLE HEART

MAY YOU LOVE PEOPLE

MAY YOU HAVE PROMISE

MAY YOU TAKE YOUR TIME

AMEN

DECREE:

YOU RUN INTO YOUR DAY WITH JOY

YOU ARE CONFIDENT

YOU ARE STRONG

YOU ARE HEALTHY

YOU LOVE THE LORD

FACT:

FASTING MAKES YOU UNSTOPPABLE

INSPIRATION:

YOU HELP MANY

Destiny Come Forth

August 23

PRAYER:

MAY YOU BE CHEERFUL

MAY YOU LIGHT UP

MAY YOU SHINE

MAY YOU DIG IN

MAY YOU HAVE FUN

AMEN

DECREE:

YOU ARE DEAR TO GOD

GOD LOVES YOU SO MUCH

YOU BRING GOD JOY

GOD IS IMPRESSED WITH YOU

YOU ALWAYS LOOK GOOD TO GOD

FACT:

FASTING BRINGS ANSWERS

INSPIRATION:

BELIEVE FOR THE BEST

Destiny Come Forth

August 24

PRAYER:

MAY YOU BE ENTHUSED

MAY YOU BE HOPEFUL

MAY YOU SEE GOD EVERYWHERE

MAY YOU TRUST IN GOD'S PLAN

MAY YOU SPEAK PROSPERITY

AMEN

DECREE:

YOU INSPIRE OTHERS

YOU ARE AN ORIGINAL

YOU WERE CREATED FOR GREATNESS

YOU ARE CREATIVE

YOU SHINE GOD'S LIGHT

FACT:

FASTING PUTS A LOVING HEART IN YOU

INSPIRATION:

THE BEST IS STILL COMING

Destiny Come Forth

August 25

PRAYER:

MAY YOU FELLOWSHIP WITH GOD

MAY YOU BECOME MORE LIKE GOD EVERY DAY

MAY GOD INVEST IN YOU

MAY YOU SEE YOUR PROGRESS

MAY YOU FEEL SIGNIFICANT

AMEN

DECREE:

YOU LOOK INTO THE DAY WITH HIGH EXPECTATION

YOU TAKE GOOD CARE OF YOURSELF

YOU ARE BELIEVING FOR THE BEST

YOU ARE STEADFAST

YOU ARE SECURE IN YOUR THINKING

FACT:

FASTING SHOWS VICTORY

INSPIRATION:

AGREE WITH HEAVEN

Destiny Come Forth

August 26

PRAYER:

MAY YOU BE FULL OF ENERGY

MAY YOU BE FOCUSED

MAY YOU BELIEVE YOU CAN DO IT

MAY YOU TAKE TERRITORY

MAY YOU GAIN GROUND

AMEN

DECREE:

YOU ARE OPTIMISTIC

YOU LOOK FOR THE GOOD

YOU HELP OTHERS SEE THE POSITIVE SIDE

YOUR CUP OVERFLOWS

YOU HAVE MORE THAN ENOUGH

FACT:

FASTING GIVES AND GIVES

INSPIRATION:

JUMP FOR JOY

Destiny Come Forth

August 27

PRAYER:

MAY YOU BE AWAKE

MAY YOU HAVE SOMETHING TO SAY

MAY YOU KNOW THAT YOUR VOICE MATTERS

MAY YOU SOUND THE ALARM

MAY YOU PREPARE THE WAY

AMEN

DECREE:

YOU REJOICE

YOU RELISH IN THE TRUTH

YOU ARE CONFIDENT

YOU STAND STRONG

YOU PUSH THROUGH

FACT:

FASTING HELPS

INSPIRATION:

HOLD TIGHT TO GOD FOR HE NEVER FAILS

August 28

PRAYER:

MAY YOU BE A BLESSING TODAY

MAY YOU LOOK FOR GOLDEN OPPORTUNITIES

MAY YOU COURAGEOUSLY SHARE YOUR FAITH

MAY YOU MENTOR MANY

MAY YOU GO OUT OF YOUR WAY TO HELP PEOPLE

AMEN

DECREE:

GOD LOVES YOU

YOU ARE HIS PRIZE

YOU WERE CREATED WITH HIS LOVING HANDS

YOU LOOK JUST LIKE HIM

YOU ARE FILLED WITH GLORIOUS POTENTIAL

AMEN

FACT:

FASTING KICK STARTS YOUR DESTINY

INSPIRATION:

GOD BLESSES YOU TO BE A BLESSING

Destiny Come Forth

August 29

PRAYER:

MAY YOU FIND YOUR PURPOSE

MAY YOU MOVE INTO YOUR DESTINY

MAY YOU HELP OTHER PEOPLE FIND GOD

MAY YOU SEEK AFTER GOD'S BEST

MAY YOU CONTINUE TO MATURE

AMEN

DECREE:

YOU ARE A CHILD OF GOD ALMIGHTY

YOUR INHERITANCE IS RICH

YOU ARE UNSTOPPABLE

GOD IS BACKING YOU UP

YOU CAN DO GREAT THINGS

FACT:

FASTING PURIFIES THE HEART

INSPIRATION:

LOVE GOD WITH YOUR LIFE

Destiny Come Forth

August 30

PRAYER:

MAY YOU WALK IN FREEDOM

MAY YOU LET IT ALL GO

MAY YOU TRUST GOD WITH RECOMPENSE

MAY YOU STAY CONTENT

MAY YOU ENJOY EVERY STAGE OF THIS LIFE

AMEN

DECREE:

GOD FILLS IN YOUR GAPS

YOU ARE COMPLETE

YOU SHARE

YOU HAVE COMPASSION

YOUR HEART IS HAPPY

FACT:

FASTING GIVES YOUR STEPS TRACTION

INSPIRATION:

GOD IS FAIR AND KNOWS ALL

Destiny Come Forth

August 31

PRAYER:

MAY YOU ENJOY YOUR DAY

MAY YOU KEEP YOUR GOALS BEFORE YOU

MAY YOU RUN FOR THE VICTORY

MAY YOU SHARE YOUR JOY

MAY YOU BELIEVE THE TRUTH

AMEN

DECREE:

YOU ARE ALIVE AND DOING WELL

YOU LIVE LIFE TO THE FULLEST

YOU BRING HEAVEN TO EARTH EVERY DAY

YOU CELEBRATE WITH GOD

YOU ARE IN A GOOD MOOD

FACT:

FASTING MOVES YOU FORWARD

INSPIRATION:

WE ARE ALL DIFFERENT SO BE DIFFERENT

September 1

PRAYER:

MAY YOU USE YOUR AUTHORITY

MAY YOU MAKE THE MOST OF WHAT YOU HAVE

MAY YOU ENJOY YOUR LIFE

MAY YOU HELP OTHERS

MAY YOU BE HAPPY

AMEN

DECREE:

YOU ARE ON THE WINNING TEAM

YOU ARE A GREAT LEADER

YOU CHEER LOUD

YOU LIFT OTHERS UP

ANGELS APPLAUD YOUR EFFORT

FACT:

FASTING LIFTS YOU UP

INSPIRATION:

HEAVEN KNOWS YOUR NAME

Destiny Come Forth

September 2

PRAYER:

MAY YOU NEVER RUN OUT OF NICE THINGS TO SAY

MAY YOU ALWAYS BE READY TO GIVE

MAY YOU ENCOURAGE OTHERS

MAY YOU LEND A HELPING HAND

MAY YOU TAKE TIME TO CARE

AMEN

DECREE:

YOU ARE SET APART FOR GOOD THINGS

YOU ARE TARGETED

YOU ARE POSITIVE

YOU ARE ABSOLUTE

YOU ARE UNLIMITED

FACT:

FASTING COMMANDS VICTORY

INSPIRATION:

YOU ARE A WINNER

Destiny Come Forth

September 3

PRAYER:

MAY YOU FEEL PRICELESS

MAY YOU KNOW YOU ARE IRREPLACEABLE

MAY YOU BE AN OVERCOMER

MAY YOU SPEND TIME WITH GOD TODAY

MAY YOU RUN FORWARD

AMEN

DECREE:

YOU ARE SECURE

YOU ARE SAFE IN GOD

YOU ARE SOLID

YOU ARE LOVED

YOU ARE GOD'S CHILD

FACT:

FASTING STRENGTHENS YOUR RELATIONSHIP WITH GOD

INSPIRATION:

GO FORWARD WITH STRENGTH

Destiny Come Forth

September 4

PRAYER:

MAY YOU BE SOLID

MAY YOU BE SECURE

MAY YOU BE A GOOD STEWARD

MAY YOU CONQUER

MAY YOU GO FORTH

AMEN

DECREE:

YOU ARE SPECIAL

YOU ARE SPECIAL TO GOD

YOU ARE SPECIAL TO MANY

YOU ARE UNIQUE

YOU HAVE FLARE

FACT:

FASTING ADMIRES GOD

INSPIRATION:

LEAP INTO THE DAY

September 5

PRAYER:

MAY YOU BE BRAVE

MAY YOU BE COURAGEOUS

MAY YOU BE FOCUSED

MAY YOU BE CONFIDENT

MAY YOU ACHIEVE VICTORY

AMEN

DECREE:

YOU ARE GRACEFUL

YOU CAN FORGIVE

YOU REDEEM

YOU HAVE GREAT FAITH

YOU EXPECT MIRACLES

FACT:

FASTING MAKES YOU ABLE

INSPIRATION:

LOVE EVERYONE

Destiny Come Forth

September 6

PRAYER:

MAY YOU BE A HOLY PACKAGE

MAY YOU BE LIT UP

MAY YOU BE PROTECTED BY GOD

MAY YOU SHINE

MAY YOU MAKE PEOPLE HAPPY

AMEN

DECREE:

YOU ARE FOCUSED

YOU ARE WELL TRAINED

YOU ARE FRIENDLY

YOU ARE ENERGETIC

YOU ARE SUCH A BLESSING

FACT:

FASTING RADIATES LOVE

INSPIRATION:

GET PLUGGED IN

Destiny Come Forth

September 7

PRAYER:

MAY YOU WALK IN FAITH

MAY YOU BELIEVE IN OTHERS

MAY YOU SET AN EXAMPLE

MAY YOU DEVELOP YOUR CHARACTER

MAY GOD BLESS YOUR LIFE

AMEN

DECREE:

YOU ARE MORE THAN ENOUGH

YOU ARE DEVELOPING A NEW WAY

YOU ARE A CHAIN BREAKER

YOU SET OTHERS FREE WITH YOUR FREEDOM

YOU ARE A FRIEND OF GOD

FACT:

FASTING BRINGS GOD CLOSER

INSPIRATION:

DO WHAT YOU CAN

Destiny Come Forth

September 8

PRAYER:

MAY YOU USE YOUR GOD GIVEN AUTHORITY

MAY YOU CREATE A DIRECT PATH TO YOUR DESTINY

MAY YOU TAKE CHARGE

MAY YOU STAY POTENT

MAY YOU IMPACT YOUR SPHERE

AMEN

DECREE:

YOU TAKE HOLD OF YOUR LIFE

YOU PRESENT EVERYTHING TO GOD

GOD BLESSES YOUR LIFE

YOU ARE IN A POSITION OF GREAT AUTHORITY

ALL OF HEAVEN CHEERS FOR YOU

FACT:

FASTING BEFRIENDS GOD

INSPIRATION:

BE THE STORM

Destiny Come Forth

September 9

PRAYER:

MAY YOU BE DEEP

MAY YOU BE REVELATORY

MAY YOU BE CLEAR

MAY YOU DEMONSTRATE LOVE

MAY YOU BE OPEN

AMEN

DECREE:

YOU ARE INTELLECTUAL

YOU MAKE PEOPLE DOUBLE TAKE

YOU STAND OUT

YOU CHANGE THE ATMOSPHERE

YOU ARE A HOLY MAGNET

FACT:

FASTING ILLUMINATES VICTORY

INSPIRATION:

YOU ARE DESTINED TO RISE

Destiny Come Forth

September 10

PRAYER:

MAY YOU FEEL LOVED

MAY YOU BE A FEARLESS LEADER

MAY YOU BELIEVE

MAY YOU DO ALL THINGS

MAY YOU PRESS ON

AMEN

DECREE:

YOU ARE MADE IN THE IMAGE OF GOD

YOU ARE CREATIVE

YOU ARE LOVING

YOU CAN FORGIVE ALL

YOU THINK BIG

FACT:

FASTING LOOKS UP

INSPIRATION:

GO FOR IT

Destiny Come Forth

September 11

PRAYER:

MAY YOU HAVE GOOD INTENTIONS

MAY YOU KNOW YOU ARE CHOSEN FOR GREAT THINGS

MAY YOU FIT IN

MAY YOU BE COMFORTED

MAY YOU BE SINCERE

AMEN

DECREE:

YOU ARE HIGH QUALITY

YOU ARE THE BEST

YOU ARE A GOD EXAMPLE

YOU ARE BRIGHT

YOU ARE SWEET

FACT:

FASTING BRIGHTENS THE DARKNESS

INSPIRATION:

HAVE A GOD DAY

Destiny Come Forth

September 12

PRAYER:

MAY YOU BE STRONG

MAY YOU BE COURAGEOUS

MAY YOU BE LOVABLE

MAY YOU FEEL VALUED

MAY YOU GLOW

AMEN

DECREE:

YOU CAN DO IT

GOD IS PLEASED WITH YOU

YOU ARE HOLY TERRITORY

YOU ARE ANOINTED

YOU ARE VICTORIOUS

FACT:

FASTING APPOINTS ANOINTING

INSPIRATION:

BE POWERFUL

Destiny Come Forth

September 13

PRAYER:

MAY YOU BE OPTIMISTIC

MAY YOU BE ENTHUSED

MAY YOU BE RELEVANT

MAY YOU BE JUSTIFIED

MAY YOU BE REDEEMED

AMEN

DECREE:

YOU ARE SIGNIFICANT

YOU IMPACT LIVES

YOU ARE WONDERFUL

YOU ARE FAITHFUL

YOU ARE HELD

FACT:

FASTING INCREASES TRUST

INSPIRATION:

BE REVIVED

Destiny Come Forth

September 14

PRAYER:

MAY YOU BE BLESSED

MAY YOU HAVE A GREAT DAY

MAY YOU ENJOY REST

MAY YOU BE A VALUABLE ASSET

MAY YOU BE INVINCIBLE

AMEN

DECREE:

YOU ARE COOL

YOU ARE CALM

YOU ARE PEACEFUL

YOU ARE SUSTAINED

YOUR LEGACY WILL REMAIN

FACT:

FASTING REVERES GOD

INSPIRATION:

BE MERITORIOUS

Destiny Come Forth

September 15

PRAYER:

MAY YOU BE COMPASSIONATE

MAY YOU BE GRACIOUS

MAY YOU BE SLOW TO ANGER

MAY YOU BE FULL OF FORGIVENESS

MAY YOU BE ABOUNDING IN LOVE

AMEN

DECREE:

YOU ARE SIGNIFICANT

YOU ARE SWEET

YOU ARE ON TOP

YOU ARE LOVED

YOU ARE BLESSED

FACT:

FASTING IS HIGHLY APPRECIATED BY GOD

INSPIRATION:

THE HOLY SPIRIT IS A GREAT HELPER

Destiny Come Forth

September 16

PRAYER:

MAY YOU BE EQUIPPED

MAY YOU BE WELL TRAINED

MAY YOU BE RESTED UP

MAY YOU BE STURDY

MAY YOU BE VOCAL

AMEN

DECREE:

YOU ARE MOTIVATED

YOU ARE HEALTHY

YOU ARE SOPHISTICATED

YOU ARE SINCERE

YOU HAVE HIGH VALUES

FACT:

FASTING HONORS GOD

INSPIRATION:

GO FOR GREATNESS

Destiny Come Forth

September 17

PRAYER:

MAY GOD BLESS YOU

MAY YOU ACHIEVE OVERALL HAPPINESS

MAY YOU HAVE JOY

MAY YOU GO FORTH IN VICTORY

MAY YOU BE SUCCESSFUL

AMEN

DECREE:

YOU ARE THANKFUL

YOU ARE GIVING

YOU ARE LOVED

YOU ARE WARM

YOU ARE FRIENDLY

FACT:

FASTING IS EXPECTANT

INSPIRATION:

BE MORE LIKE CHRIST

Destiny Come Forth

September 18

PRAYER:

MAY YOU CREATE HARMONY

MAY YOU ENJOY PEACE TODAY

MAY YOU FIND YOUR RHYTHM

MAY YOU STAND UP AND BE COUNTED

MAY YOU MAKE YOUR LIFE COUNT

AMEN

DECREE:

YOU ARE FUN

YOU ARE LIKE SUNSHINE

YOU WARM PEOPLE UP

YOU ARE FULL OF JOY

YOU BURST FORTH

FACT:

FASTING STRUCTURES YOUR WEEK

INSPIRATION:

FIX WHAT YOU CAN FIX

Destiny Come Forth

September 19

PRAYER:

MAY YOU MOVE SALVATION FORWARD TODAY

MAY YOU USE YOUR SHIELD OF FAITH

MAY YOU WIELD THE SWORD OF THE LORD

MAY YOU RUN INTO YOUR SHOES OF PEACE

MAY YOU BELT ON THE TRUTH WITH RIGHTEOUSNESS

AMEN

DECREE:

YOU ARE BOLD

YOU ARE CONFIDENT

YOU ARE WORTH THE PRICE GOD PAID

YOU ARE SOLD OUT

YOUR CAUSE CALLS YOU

FACT:

REGULAR FASTING MAKES SENSE IN MANY WAYS

INSPIRATION:

GOD IS RECRUITING

Destiny Come Forth

September 20

PRAYER:

MAY YOU BE CELEBRATED

MAY YOU BE ENCOURAGED

MAY YOU BE EXUBERANT

MAY YOU BE TENACIOUS

MAY YOU BE DIGNIFIED

AMEN

DECREE:

YOU ARE CHOSEN FOR GREATNESS

YOU ARE MOVING FORWARD

YOU ARE A CATALYST

YOU ARE FULL OF MOMENTUM

YOU ARE ICONIC

FACT:

FASTING MAKES YOU SATISFIED

INSPIRATION:

BE EAGER FOR MORE

Destiny Come Forth

September 21

PRAYER:

MAY YOU BE STRONG

MAY YOU BE A FINISHER

MAY YOU DO WELL IN ALL THINGS

MAY YOU WALK IN YOUR GIFTINGS

MAY YOU BE HOPEFUL

AMEN

DECREE:

YOU ARE FREE INDEED

YOU ARE RANSOMED

YOU KNOW THE TRUTH

YOU KNOW THE WAY

YOU KNOW THE LIGHT

FACT:

FASTING OPENS DOORS FOR YOU

INSPIRATION:

BE DETERMINED TO LOVE

Destiny Come Forth

September 22

PRAYER:

MAY YOU BE CALM

MAY YOU BE UNWAVERING IN YOUR FAITH

MAY YOU BE A LIGHT

MAY YOU BE VIVID

MAY YOU BE FASCINATING

AMEN

DECREE:

YOU ARE UNIQUE

YOU ARE IRREPLACEABLE

YOU ARE CLEAR

YOU ARE FLAMBOYANT

YOU ARE IRRESISTIBLE

FACT:

FASTING IS HOLY

INSPIRATION:

YOU ARE CREATED IN GOD'S IMAGE

Destiny Come Forth

September 23

PRAYER:

MAY YOU BE FOCUSED

MAY YOU BE SURE

MAY YOU BE READY

MAY YOU SUCCEED WITH SPEED

MAY YOU BE HEALTHY

AMEN

DECREE:

YOU ARE ONE OF GOD'S GREATS

YOU ARE PERFECT

YOU ARE PERFECTED BY GOD

YOU ARE LOVED

YOU ARE CARED ABOUT

FACT:

FASTING IS A TRUE JOY

INSPIRATION:

GO AND MAKE A DIFFERENCE

Destiny Come Forth

September 24

PRAYER:

MAY YOU FIX YOUR EYES ON THE TRUTH

MAY YOU BE HONORABLE

MAY YOU KNOW WHAT IS RIGHT

MAY YOU BE PURIFIED

MAY YOU BE LOVED

AMEN

DECREE:

YOU ARE LOVING

YOU ARE JOYFUL

YOU ARE PEACEFUL

YOU ARE PATIENT

YOU ARE GENTLE

FACT:

FASTING IS ADMIRED

INSPIRATION:

GOD KNOWS THE FAITHFUL

Destiny Come Forth

September 25

PRAYER:

MAY YOU BE COURAGEOUS

MAY YOU BE IN TUNE

MAY YOU BE STRATEGIC

MAY YOU BE HOLY

MAY YOU BE STRENGTHENED

AMEN

DECREE:

YOU ARE TRIUMPHANT

YOU ARE STRONG

YOU ARE FEARLESS

YOU ARE FAITHFUL

YOU ARE STOUT

FACT:

FASTING IS IMPORTANT TO GOD

INSPIRATION:

CHRIST'S BODY IS STRONGER TOGETHER

Destiny Come Forth

September 26

PRAYER:

MAY YOU BE HOPEFUL

MAY YOU BE PEACEFUL

MAY YOU BE HOLY

MAY YOU BE COMFORTED

MAY YOU BE HIGHLY FAVORED

AMEN

DECREE:

YOU ARE SERENE

YOU ARE CALM

YOU ARE COMPOSED

YOU ARE FOCUSED

YOU ARE GOAL ORIENTED

FACT:

FASTING MAKES YOU IMMOVABLE

INSPIRATION:

YOU CAN DO THIS

Destiny Come Forth

September 27

PRAYER:

MAY YOU GROW IN YOUR FAITH

MAY YOU WALK IN LOVE

MAY YOUR STEPS SPELL DIGNITY

MAY YOU BRING HEAVENLY THINGS TO EARTH

MAY GOD FLOW THROUGH YOU

AMEN

DECREE:

YOU ARE A GOOD STEWARD

YOU TAKE CARE OF WHAT YOU HAVE

YOU SHARE YOUR BLESSINGS WITH OTHERS

YOUR RESOURCES ARE MULTIPLIED BY GOD

YOU HAVE NO FEAR

FACT:

FASTING PROTECTS YOUR NATION

INSPIRATION:

GOD USES EVERYONE

Destiny Come Forth

September 28

PRAYER:

MAY YOU FIND EXTRA STRENGTH IN GOD

MAY YOU HELP STRENGTHEN OTHERS

MAY THE JOY OF GOD FILL YOU AFRESH TODAY

MAY YOU SEE THINGS WITH A HOLY PERSPECTIVE

MAY YOU START FRESH

AMEN

DECREE:

YOU ARE ON THE TOP

YOU STAY ON THE TOP

GOD HAS BLESSED YOU

YOU ALWAYS LAND UP ON YOUR FEET

YOU HELP OTHER PEOPLE STAND UP TOO

FACT:

FASTING FILLS YOUR SPIRITUAL TANK

INSPIRATION:

REACH OUT FROM YOUR COMFORT ZONE

Destiny Come Forth

September 29

PRAYER:

MAY YOU REACH FOR THE LOST

MAY YOU FIND YOUR CALLING

MAY YOU SHOW OTHERS THE WAY TO GO

MAY YOU BE THE HANDS OF GOD

MAY GOD BE DELIGHTED IN YOU

DECREE:

YOU HEAR THE TRUTH FROM GOD

YOU PROCLAIM IT TO THE NATIONS

YOU STAY HOPEFUL

YOU LOVE YOUR LIFE

YOU APPRECIATE WHAT YOU HAVE

FACT:

FASTING UNITES COUNTRIES

INSPIRATION:

GOD IS SO PROUD OF YOU

Destiny Come Forth

September 30

PRAYER:

MAY YOU FEEL QUALIFIED

MAY YOU MAKE GOD TANGIBLE

MAY YOU BE NETWORKED

MAY YOU BE ESTEEMED

MAY YOU BE YOUR DYNAMIC SELF

AMEN

DECREE:

YOU ARE HAPPY

YOU ARE WHOLE

YOU ARE SAFE

YOU ARE SOUND

YOU ARE STEADY

FACT:

FASTING POSITIONS YOU TO WIN

INSPIRATION:

YOU ARE GOD'S BELOVED PRIZE

Destiny Come Forth

October 1

PRAYER:

MAY YOU BE EXTRAORDINARY

MAY YOU FEEL EXQUISITE

MAY YOU BE DISTINCT

MAY YOU BE SHARP

MAY YOU BE WISE

AMEN

DECREE:

YOU ARE PRICELESS

YOU ARE A TREASURE

YOU ARE SIGNIFICANT

YOU ARE TRUSTED

YOU ARE VALIANT

FACT:

FASTING HARVESTS GOLD

INSPIRATION:

LET GOD BE YOUR MAIN PRIORITY

Destiny Come Forth

October 2

PRAYER:

MAY YOU BE STEADY

MAY YOU BE READY

MAY YOU BE SOLID

MAY YOU BE FOCUSED

MAY YOU BE WELL POISED

AMEN

DECREE:

GOD IS WITH YOU

YOU ARE CHOSEN

YOU ARE GREAT

YOU ARE DETERMINED

YOU SIGNIFY GOD'S GREATNESS

FACT:

FASTING BREAKS CHAINS

INSPIRATION:

OVERCOME

Destiny Come Forth

October 3

PRAYER:

MAY YOU BE ON PACE

MAY YOU BE ON TARGET

MAY YOU DO ALL THINGS WELL

MAY YOU FEEL APPRECIATED

MAY YOU HAVE JOY

DECREE:

YOU ARE INSPIRING

YOU ARE ZESTFUL

YOU ARE EXUBERANT

YOU ARE FREE

YOU ARE A GREAT FRIEND

FACT:

FASTING PLEASES GOD

INSPIRATION:

TEACH BY YOUR EXAMPLE

Destiny Come Forth

October 4

PRAYER:

MAY YOU BE FULL OF GOD

MAY YOU BE LOYAL

MAY YOU BE FAITHFUL

MAY YOU BE CHEERFUL

MAY YOU BE FUN LOVING

AMEN

DECREE:

YOU ARE LOVED

YOU ARE HEALTHY

YOU ARE CONFIDENT

YOU ARE PROFOUND

YOU CAN DO IT

FACT:

FASTING SEEKS DIVINE HEALTH

INSPIRATION:

YOU WILL BE REWARDED

Destiny Come Forth

October 5

PRAYER:

MAY YOU BE STRAIGHTFORWARD

MAY YOU FEEL VALUED

MAY YOU FEEL IMPORTANT

MAY YOU BE JOYFUL

MAY YOU HAVE PEACE

AMEN

DECREE:

YOU ARE AWESOME

YOU ARE FEARLESS

YOU ARE UPRIGHT

YOU ARE OUTSTANDING

YOU ARE ELITE

FACT:

FASTING ENHANCES GLORY

INSPIRATION:

SPEAKING LIFE BRINGS LIFE

Destiny Come Forth

October 6

PRAYER:

MAY YOU OPEN YOUR MIND

MAY GOD INHABIT YOUR THOUGHTS

MAY YOUR ACTIONS ALIGN WITH GOD'S PLAN

MAY YOU REAP GOOD THINGS

MAY YOUR HARVEST BE PLENTIFUL

AMEN

DECREE:

YOU ARE FULL OF GOODNESS

YOU ARE GOOD TO ALL

YOU REACH FOR THE BEST

YOU LIVE A WELL BALANCED LIFE

YOU ARE GOOD

FACT:

FASTING KEEPS YOU FLOATING

INSPIRATION:

GOD LOVES YOUR HEART

Destiny Come Forth

October 7

PRAYER:

MAY YOU WALK IN THE SUPERNATURAL

MAY YOU HAVE FUN

MAY YOU GIVE LIFE

MAY YOU BE OPEN TO NEW THINGS

MAY YOU STAY FOCUSED

AMEN

DECREE:

YOU CAN DO IT

YOU ARE GIFTED

YOU ARE WISE

YOU ARE CHERISHED

YOU ARE APPRECIATED

FACT:

FASTING IS UPRIGHT

INSPIRATION:

STAND STRONG

Destiny Come Forth

October 7

PRAYER:

MAY YOU BE STRONG

MAY YOU BE SMART

MAY YOU FEEL LOVE

MAY YOU BE RESPECTABLE

MAY YOU BE BLESSED

AMEN

DECREE:

YOU ARE SAVED

YOU ARE SECURE

YOU ARE SAFE

YOU ARE AN ICON

YOU ARE KIND

FACT:

FASTING PROPELS YOU FORWARD

INSPIRATION:

JESUS LOVES EVERYONE AND SO SHOULD YOU

Destiny Come Forth

October 8

PRAYER:

MAY YOU BE JOYFUL

MAY YOU BE WHOLE

MAY YOU BE DIGNIFIED

MAY YOU KNOW YOUR VALUE

MAY YOU WALK IN LOVE

AMEN

DECREE:

YOU ARE FULL OF FAITH

YOU CAN DO IT ALL

YOU HAVE WILL POWER

YOU ARE CHOSEN

YOU ARE ABLE

FACT:

FASTING DELIVERS

INSPIRATION:

LEAD OTHERS TODAY

Destiny Come Forth

October 9

PRAYER:

MAY YOU FIND YOUR PLACE

MAY YOU SEEK GOD'S FACE

MAY YOU ALIGN WITH WHAT IS RIGHT

MAY YOU LET GOD FIGHT FOR YOU

MAY YOU BREAKTHROUGH

AMEN

DECREE:

YOU ARE A CHAMPION OF THE FAITH

YOU ARE A WEAPON AGAINST THE DARKNESS

YOU ARE BRIGHT LIKE A HIGH BEAM

GOD PLACES YOU STRATEGICALLY

PREPARE FOR YOUR PROSPERITY

FACT:

FASTING OPENS YOUR EYES

INSPIRATION:

LEARN FROM THE PEOPLE, PLACES, AND THINGS IN FRONT OF YOU

Destiny Come Forth

October 10

PREPARE:

MAY YOU LIVE TO LOVE

MAY YOU DO YOUR BEST

MAY YOU WALK IN TOTAL FORGIVENESS

MAY YOU BE MORE LIKE THE LORD

MAY YOU SET PEOPLE FREE

DECREE:

YOU CAN OVERCOME

YOU HAVE DONE IT BEFORE

YOU CAN DO IT AGAIN

GOD HELPS YOU

YOU HELP OTHER PEOPLE

FACT:

FASTING FINDS REST

INSPIRATION:

BE WRAPPED UP IN GOD'S LOVE

Destiny Come Forth

October 11

PRAYER:

MAY YOU BE BLESSED

MAY GOD PROTECT YOU

MAY GOD SMILE AT YOU

MAY GOD BE GRACIOUS TO YOU

MAY GOD FAVOR YOU

DECREE:

YOU ARE ON TOP

YOU ARE ABOVE

YOU ARE IN FRONT

YOU ARE OVER IT

YOU CLIMB EVEN HIGHER

FACT:

FASTING BLESSES YOUR FUTURE

INSPIRATION:

GOD GIVES PEACE

Destiny Come Forth

October 12

PREPARE:

MAY YOU BE FREE INDEED

MAY YOU LIBERATE OTHERS

MAY YOU COUNT YOUR BLESSINGS

MY YOU BE A BLESSING TO OTHERS

MAY YOU STAY POSITIVE

AMEN

DECREE:

YOU LOVE GOD

YOU LOVE PEOPLE

YOU LOVE YOUR LIFE

YOU ENCOURAGE OTHERS

YOU DO GREAT THINGS

FACT:

FASTING ENHANCES LOVE

INSPIRATION:

BE A FISHER OF MEN

Destiny Come Forth

October 13

PRAYER:

MAY YOU DO WHAT YOU GOTTA DO

MAY YOU MAKE A LIST

MAY YOU COMPLETE EVERYTHING THAT MUST BE DONE

MAY YOU KEEP YOUR GOALS BEFORE YOU

MAY YOU LIVE IN THE FINISHED LAND

AMEN

DECREE:

GOD SPEAKS TO YOU

YOU SIT AND LISTEN TO GOD

YOU GIVE GOD YOUR TIME

YOU GIVE GOD YOUR TALENTS

YOU ASK GOD TO USE YOU

FACT:

FASTING REGULATES YOUR LIFE

INSPIRATION:

STAY STEADY

Destiny Come Forth

October 14

PRAYER:

MAY YOU PLAN ON MEETING WITH GOD

MAY GOD ORDER YOUR STEPS

MAY YOU WALK FORWARD BOLDLY

MAY YOU WALK WITH LOVE

MAY YOU HEAR CLEARLY

AMEN

DECREE:

YOU HEAR GOD CLEARLY

YOU SEE GOD'S PLAN

YOU MAKE THINGS CLEAR FOR OTHERS

YOU CARE ABOUT EVERYONE

YOU USE YOUR GIFTS

FACT:

FASTING FIGHTS FOR TRUTH

INSPIRATION:

KNOWING THE BIBLE IS KEY

Destiny Come Forth

October 15

PRAYER:

MAY YOU BE WISE

MAY YOU SEEK THE LORD

MAY YOU BRING HIM YOUR GIFTS

MAY YOU TELL EVERYONE YOU KNOW

MAY YOU SHINE HIS LIGHT

AMEN

DECREE:

YOU ARE PUMPED UP

YOU ARE ALWAYS READY FOR MORE

YOU SEEK THE LORD WITH DILIGENCE

YOU ARE FAITH FULL

YOU USE YOUR ZEAL WISELY

FACT:

FASTING BREAKS YOU THROUGH

INSPIRATION:

YOU ARE WORTHWHILE

Destiny Come Forth

October 16

PRAYER:

MAY YOU FIND MOMENTUM

MAY YOU PRESS THROUGH

MAY YOU STAY MOTIVATED

MAY YOU FEEL GOD'S POWER

MAY YOU STAY OPTIMISTIC

AMEN

DECREE:

YOU SUCCEED WITH SPEED

GOD BREAKS THE WIND FOR YOU

GOD LIFTS YOU UP

YOU GO HIGHER AND HIGHER

YOU RISE TO WIN

FACT:

FASTING STRENGTHENS YOUR FORTITUDE

INSPIRATION:

GOD PROVIDES

Destiny Come Forth

October 17

PRAYER:

MAY YOU STAY REFRESHED

MAY YOU REFRESH OTHERS

MAY YOU FIND GOD'S PATH OF BLESSING

MAY YOU TREASURE GOD'S LOVE

MAY YOU SHARE GOD'S TREASURE

AMEN

DECREE:

YOU ARE FULL OF JOY

YOU HAVE UNSHAKABLE FAITH

YOU HAVE SO MUCH TO BE THANKFUL FOR

YOU ARE PEACE DRIVEN

YOU ARE IN AN OASIS OF GRATITUDE

FACT:

FASTING STRAIGHTENS THINGS OUT

INSPIRATION:

KEEP IT MOVING

Destiny Come Forth

October 18

PRAYER:

MAY THE WISDOM OF GOD GUIDE YOU

MAY YOU STAY FOCUSSED

MAY YOU PERSEVERE THROUGH THE TOUGH TIMES

MAY YOU LEND A HELPING HAND TO OTHERS

MAY YOU CONNECT TO THEM WITH GENUINE AFFECTION

AMEN

DECREE:

YOU ARE SOLID

YOU ARE FULL OF COMPASSION

YOU HAVE WISDOM BEYOND YOUR YEARS

THE GOOD THAT YOU HAVE DONE IS COMING BACK TO YOU

GREAT IS YOUR REWARD

FACT:

FASTING IS A GAME CHANGER

INSPIRATION:

LOOK FOR THE BIG PICTURE

Destiny Come Forth

October 19

PRAYER:

MAY YOU LOOK TO GOD FOR ALL OF THE ANSWERS

MAY YOU SHARE HIS RESPONSES

MAY YOU BUILD OTHER PEOPLE UP

MAY YOU MOVE FORWARD WITH SKILL

MAY YOU STRIVE TO THRIVE

AMEN

DECREE:

YOU STAND TALL

YOU ARE ENOUGH

YOU HOLD YOUR HEAD HIGH

YOUR CUP OVERFLOWS

YOU ARE A POWERFUL VESSEL OF GOD

FACT:

FASTING DEVELOPS YOUR WILLPOWER

INSPIRATION:

PUMPED UP AND ON POINT

Destiny Come Forth

October 20

PRAYER:

MAY YOU THINK THINGS THROUGH

MAY YOU GAIN GOD'S PERSPECTIVE

MAY YOU SEE THE BEST

MAY YOU ENJOY THIS DAY

MAY YOU REST WELL

AMEN

DECREE:

YOU ARE SWEET

YOU ARE CHERISHED

YOU ARE THOUGHT HIGHLY OF

PEOPLE LOOK UP TO YOU

YOU HAVE GAINED HOLY INSIGHT

FACT:

FASTING SPEEDS UP VICTORY

INSPIRATION:

PICK UP THE BIBLE AND DO NOT PUT IT DOWN

Destiny Come Forth

October 21

PRAYER:

MAY YOU RECEIVE RESTITUTION

MAY YOU BECOME A FORCE OF RESTORATION

MAY YOU BELIEVE FOR THE BEST

MAY YOU ADHERE TO THE TRUTH

MAY YOU SEEK GOD FOR EVERYTHING

AMEN

DECREE:

YOU ARE HAPPY

YOU ARE JOYFUL ON THE INSIDE

YOU BRING WARMTH TO THE ATMOSPHERE

YOU SHIFT DESTINY

YOU STAY WITH GOD

FACT:

FASTING FINDS REFUGE

INSPIRATION:

BE YOUR BEST

Destiny Come Forth

October 22

PRAYER:

MAY YOU GO INTO TODAY FEELING STRONG

MAY YOU FIND PEACE

MAY YOU FIND YOUR LANE

MAY YOU FIND YOUR PURPOSE

MAY YOU HEED GOD'S CALL

AMEN

DECREE:

YOU HAVE STRONG HOPE

YOUR FAITH IS SOLID

YOU TRUST GOD WITH EVERYTHING

GOD TRUSTS YOU

YOU ARE AN ASSET

FACT:

FASTING REVIVES YOU

INSPIRATION:

SIT WITH GOD

HE IS ALWAYS THERE

Destiny Come Forth

October 23

PRAYER:

MAY YOU FIND TIME TO REST

MAY YOU TURN TOWARD GOD

MAY YOU STAY FOCUSED ON HIS LOVE

MAY YOU REMEMBER WHAT GOD DID FOR YOU

MAY YOU WHOLLY REJOICE

AMEN

DECREE:

YOU ARE HEALTHY

YOUR BODY, SOUL, AND SPIRIT WORK WELL

YOU FOLLOW GOD

YOU STAY THE COURSE

YOU KEEP MOVING ONWARD

FACT:

FASTING WINS THE RACE

INSPIRATION:

MIRACLES DO HAPPEN

Destiny Come Forth

October 24

PRAYER:

MAY YOU FIND SUPERNATURAL STRENGTH

MAY YOU GAIN MOMENTUM

MAY YOU LOOK FOR THE GOOD NEWS

MAY YOU LINK UP WITH POSITIVE PEOPLE

MAY YOU FINISH WHAT YOU START

AMEN

DECREE:

YOU ARE AN AMAZING PERSON

YOU DO AMAZING THINGS

YOU ARE SURROUNDED BY ANGELS

YOU SEARCH FOR ANSWERS

YOU MAKE QUALITY DECISIONS

FACT:

FASTING REIGNITES DREAMS

INSPIRATION:

LOOK TOWARD GOD

Destiny Come Forth

October 25

PRAYER:

MAY YOU PRESS ON

MAY YOU PRESS IN

MAY YOU STAY FOCUSED

MAY YOU LET GOD DEFINE YOU

MAY YOU STAND THE TESTS OF TIME

AMEN

DECREE:

YOU CAN DO IT

YOU HAVE INTEGRITY

YOUR CORE IS SOLID

YOU BUILD OTHER PEOPLE UP

YOU GO TO GOD

FACT:

FASTING IS A WINNER

INSPIRATION:

THERE IS A TIME FOR EVERYTHING

Destiny Come Forth

October 26

PRAYER:

MAY YOU REST IN THE ARMS OF GOD

MAY YOU GAIN STRENGTH

MAY YOU FIND PEACE TODAY

MAY YOU SMILE AND MEAN IT

MAY YOU HOPE FOR THE BEST

AMEN

DECREE:

YOU ARE FUN TO WATCH

YOU ARE A GREAT EXAMPLE

YOU DISPLAY GOD'S GOODNESS

YOUR REPUTATION SAYS IT ALL

YOU ARE A GOOD DEED DOER

FACT:

FASTING SPEEDS UP GOD'S ANSWERS TO PRAYER

INSPIRATION:

GOD DOES EVERYTHING WELL

Destiny Come Forth

October 27

PRAYER:

MAY YOU SEEK GOD FIRST

MAY YOU BECOME MORE LIKE HIM

MAY YOU LEARN MORE EVERY DAY

MAY YOU ACT LIKE JESUS

MAY YOU WALK HUMBLY

AMEN

DECREE:

YOU ARE COVERED BY GOD

GOD HAS YOUR BACK

YOU ARE SURROUNDED BY GOD'S GOODNESS

YOU FOCUS ON HIM

YOU WIN

FACT:

FASTING FINDS HIDDEN TREASURE

INSPIRATION:

THERE IS MORE THAN ONE WAY TO PRAISE THE LORD

Destiny Come Forth

October 28

PRAYER:

MAY YOU HAVE FUN TODAY

MAY YOU REFLECT ON WHAT YOU ARE GRATEFUL FOR

MAY YOU REMIND YOURSELF OF GOD'S GOODNESS

MAY YOU HEAR GOD'S LOVE TONES

MAY YOU KNOW HOW MUCH YOU ARE LOVED

AMEN

DECREE:

YOU HAVE A SWEET HEART

GOD CREATED YOU TO CARE

YOU LOVE WITH GENEROSITY

YOU FIND GOODNESS

YOU STAY HEALTHY

FACT:

FASTING GUIDES YOUR LIFE

INSPIRATION:

GOD WILL PUT YOU ON A TRAIL OF BLESSINGS AFTER A TRAIL OF TEARS

Destiny Come Forth

October 29

PRAYER:

MAY YOU WALK WITH LOVE

MAY YOU USE YOUR FAITH

MAY YOU SEEK GOD'S HEART

MAY YOU BE AT PEACE

MAY GOD CONSUME YOU

AMEN

DECREE:

GOD'S GOT YOU

YOU WALK WITH GOD HAND IN HAND

YOU FEEL SAFE

YOU FEEL LOVED

YOU ARE BEING GUIDED BY GOD

FACT:

FASTING BRINGS HEALING

INSPIRATION:

USE YOUR FAITH TO GET SOMEWHERE

Destiny Come Forth

October 30

PRAYER:

MAY YOU FIND REFUGE IN THE STRENGTH OF GOD

MAY YOU FIND PEACE

MAY YOU FIND TRUTH

MAY YOU EXCEL IN EVANGELISM

MAY YOU BOLDLY PROCLAIM THE VICTORY

AMEN

DECREE:

YOU SURROUND YOURSELF WITH GOD'S FRIENDS

YOU GO OUT OF YOUR WAY TO HELP

YOUR REWARD IS MULTIPLYING

YOUR JOY BUBBLES UP

YOU LOVE YOUR WAY TO THE TOP

FACT:

FASTING PROPELS PROSPERITY

INSPIRATION:

THE MORE YOU DO THE MORE YOU CAN DO

Destiny Come Forth

October 31

PRAYER:

MAY YOU BELIEVE FOR THE BEST

MAY YOU STRIVE FOR EXCELLENCE

MAY YOU KEEP YOUR FEET MOVING FORWARD

MAY YOU TRUST GOD WITH THE RESULTS

MAY YOU GIVE GOD ALL THE GLORY

AMEN

DECREE:

YOU ARE GIFTED

YOU ARE TALENTED

YOU OOZE WITH GOD'S GOODNESS

YOU ARE SPECIAL

YOU ARE UNIQUE

FACT:

FASTING RECIPROCATES

INSPIRATION:

MAKE SURE THAT WHAT YOU DO LOOKS LIKE THE LORD

Destiny Come Forth

November 1

PRAYER:

MAY YOU REMEMBER WHAT GOD HAS DONE IN YOUR LIFE

MAY YOU LOOK FORWARD WITH ENTHUSIASM

MAY YOU BE CONFIDENT

MAY YOU BE STRONG

MAY YOU STAY FAITHFUL

AMEN

DECREE:

YOU ARE MORE THAN ENOUGH

YOU CAN DO IT

YOU WILL MAKE IT THROUGH

YOU WILL PUSH UNTIL THE END

YOU ARE MADE IN GOD'S IMAGE

FACT:

FASTING BREAKS GENERATIONAL CHAINS

INSPIRATION:

FOCUS ON WHAT GOD IS DOING

Destiny Come Forth

November 2

PRAYER:

MAY YOUR DAY BE BRIGHT

MAY YOU SHINE EVEN BRIGHTER

MAY YOU GLISTEN WITH JOY

MAY YOU CHERISH THESE MOMENTS

MAY YOU LOOK FORWARD TO TODAY'S EVENTS

AMEN

DECREE:

YOU ARE VALUABLE

YOU ARE MADE IN GOD'S IMAGE

WALK LIKE YOU ARE GOD'S

YOU ARE AWAKE AND AWARE

YOU ARE READY

FACT:

FASTING FUELS MOTIVATION

INSPIRATION:

ROAR LOUDER THAN THE HATERS

Destiny Come Forth

November 3

PRAYER:

MAY YOU HAVE DIVINE APPOINTMENTS

MAY YOU HAVE VISITATIONS FROM GOD

MAY YOU TRUST HIS HAND

MAY YOU BELIEVE FOR THE REST

MAY YOU STAY WITH OPTIMISTIC PEOPLE

DECREE:

YOU WORK HARD

YOU STRIVE FOR GREATNESS

YOU HIT THE MARK

YOU ARE GOD'S ROYALTY

YOU ARE ALL YOU NEED TO BE

FACT:

FASTING COMPLETES YOU

INSPIRATION:

HOLD ON TO GOD'S HAND AND YOU WILL NEVER FALL

Destiny Come Forth

November 4

PRAYER:

MAY YOU FEEL SPECIAL

MAY YOU HELP OTHERS FEEL SPECIAL

MAY YOU DREAM BIG

MAY YOU ACHIEVE YOUR DREAMS

MAY YOU PURSUE GOD

AMEN

DECREE:

YOU PRESS ON

YOU CONTINUE ON THE JOURNEY BEFORE YOU

YOU MAKE WISE CHOICES

YOU SMILE BRIGHT

YOU ARE RADIANT

FACT:

FASTING PLEASES GOD

INSPIRATION:

BE A SWEET SOUND TO GOD'S EAR TODAY

Destiny Come Forth

November 5

PRAYER:

MAY YOU BRING JOY TO OTHERS

MAY YOU FOLLOW IN GOD'S FOOTSTEPS

MAY YOU FULFILL YOUR CALLING

MAY YOU REWRITE YOUR HISTORY

MAY YOU STOP DOUBTING WHO YOU ARE

AMEN

DECREE:

YOU ARE POWERFUL

YOU ARE BRAVE

YOU ARE COMPETENT

YOU ARE ABLE

YOU ARE WILLING

FACT:

FASTING CLEARS YOUR MIND

INSPIRATION:

JESUS WAS A WILLING SACRIFICE FOR YOU

Destiny Come Forth

November 6

PRAYER:

MAY YOU KEEP KEEPING ON

MAY YOU DREAM ON

MAY YOU CARRY ON

MAY YOU PRESS ON

MAY YOU GO ON AND ON

AMEN

DECREE:

YOU ARE CREATED FOR GREATNESS

YOU WILL COMPLETE YOUR DESTINY

YOU ARE ENOUGH

YOU ARE STRONGER THAN YOU KNOW

YOU ARE FORGIVEN

FACT:

FASTING HELPS YOU OUT IN THE LONG RUN

INSPIRATION:

NEVER DOUBT GOD'S ABILITY

Destiny Come Forth

November 7

PRAYER

MAY YOU BELIEVE GOD

MAY YOU MOVE FORWARD IN CONFIDENCE

MAY YOU TURN THE OTHER CHEEK

MAY YOU THINK LIKE CHRIST

MAY YOU LOVE LIKE GOD FIRST LOVED YOU

AMEN

DECREE:

YOU ARE FIERCE

YOU ARE ON FIRE FOR GOD

OTHERS CAN SEE GOD'S LOVE IN YOU

YOU GIVE MORE THAN YOU TAKE

YOU RADIATE AUTHENTICITY

FACT:

FASTING BREATHES LIFE

INSPIRATION:

BRING LOVE TO THE TABLE

Destiny Come Forth

November 8

PRAYER:

MAY YOU HOLD STEADY

MAY YOU OPEN YOUR MIND

MAY YOU HELP THOSE AROUND YOU

MAY YOU STAY GROUNDED

MAY YOU LOVE UNCONDITIONALLY

AMEN

DECREE:

YOU ARE BRIGHT

YOU ARE RIGHT

YOU ARE ALWAYS CHANGING

YOU HAVE BEEN MADE NEW IN CHRIST

YOU ARE LOVABLE

FACT:

FASTING STRENGTHENS YOUR MIND, BODY, AND SOUL

INSPIRATION:

BE A FUNNEL FOR GOD

Destiny Come Forth

November 9

PRAYER:

MAY YOU HAVE AN AMAZING DAY

MAY YOU REACH FOR GOD

MAY YOU DREAM ON

MAY YOU HOPE FOR THE BEST RESULTS

MAY YOU BELIEVE IN YOURSELF

AMEN

DECREE:

YOU ARE MIGHTY

YOU ARE MADE WHOLE

YOU ARE BRILLIANT

YOU ARE ON FIRE FOR GOD

YOU ARE AN ECHO OF GOD'S VOICE

FACT:

FASTING LETS GOD PROVE HIMSELF TO YOU

INSPIRATION:

GOD IS HERE

Destiny Come Forth

November 10

PRAYER:

MAY YOU OPEN YOUR EYES

MAY GOD'S BLESSING FALL IN YOUR LAP

MAY YOU EXPECT GREATNESS

MAY YOU LOOK TO HEAVEN FOR YOUR WORTH

MAY YOU LOVE UNCONDITIONALLY

AMEN

DECREE:

YOU ARE HOLY

YOU ARE INFORMED

YOU ARE ESTEEMED BY GOD

YOU HELP OTHERS

YOU BRING LIGHT TO THOSE AROUND YOU

FACT:

FASTING HOLDS YOU STEADY

INSPIRATION:

THE BEST STILL AWAITS

Destiny Come Forth

November 11

PRAYER:

MAY YOU STAY HOPEFUL

MAY YOU STAY JOYFUL

MAY YOU STAY AFLOAT

MAY YOU HOLD YOUR OWN

MAY YOU STAY STRONG IN YOUR FAITH

AMEN

DECREE:

YOU ARE ENOUGH SO REMEMBER THAT

YOU ARE OPEN MINDED

YOU ARE RESILIENT

YOU ARE INTENTIONAL

YOU INTIMIDATE THE ENEMY

FACT:

FASTING BRINGS STRENGTH

INSPIRATION:

YOUR TREASURE IS FOUND IN HEAVEN

Destiny Come Forth

November 12

PRAYER:

MAY YOU ENHANCE YOUR VIEW OF HEAVEN

MAY YOU SEE SIGNS AND WONDERS

MAY YOU DO JUST AS JESUS DID

MAY YOU LOVE OTHERS

MAY YOU LET OTHERS LOVE YOU

AMEN

DECREE:

YOU ARE AMAZING

YOU ARE LOYAL TO THE CAUSE

YOU ARE GOD'S CHILD

YOU HAVE AN INHERITANCE

YOU ARE BLESSED BEYOND MEASURE

FACT:

FASTING BREAKS FOOD ADDICTION

INSPIRATION:

HIT THE GAS PEDAL

Destiny Come Forth

November 13

PRAYER:

MAY YOU SMELL GOD'S HOLY FRAGRANCE

MAY YOU BE REFRESHED TODAY

MAY YOU JUST KEEP SWIMMING

MAY YOU PUSH THROUGH THE CURRENT

MAY YOU SEE IT TO THE END

AMEN

DECREE:

YOU ARE OF FUN TO BE AROUND

YOU ARE VALUABLE

YOU ARE A TREASURE

YOU ARE UNBREAKABLE

YOU ARE UNDEFEATED

FACT:

FASTING IS VALUED IN HEAVEN

INSPIRATION:

WALK IN UNCONDITIONAL FORGIVENESS

Destiny Come Forth

November 14

PRAYER:

MAY YOU SING A NEW SONG

MAY YOU STAY IN PERFECT HARMONY WITH OTHERS

MAY YOU SHOUT FOR JOY

MAY YOU MAKE THIS DAY DIFFERENT THAN THE REST

MAY YOU FIGHT FOR PEACE

AMEN

DECREE:

YOU ARE EXTRAVAGANT

YOU ARE DIFFERENT

YOU ARE HELPFUL

YOU ARE MORE THAN CAPABLE

YOU CAN DO IT AGAIN AND AGAIN

FACT:

FASTING DEVELOPS SELF CONTROL

INSPIRATION:

DO NOT DESPISE SMALL BEGINNINGS

Destiny Come Forth

November 15

PRAYER:

MAY YOU BELIEVE WHAT GOD SAYS

MAY YOU BLESS GOD'S SERVANTS

MAY YOU LOOK FOR OPPORTUNITIES TO SERVE

MAY YOU APPRECIATE WHAT YOU HAVE

MAY YOU DO YOUR BEST

AMEN

DECREE:

YOU ARE THRIVING

THIS IS YOUR TIME

THE WAIT IS OVER FOR YOU

IT IS TIME TO SHINE

YOU KNOW THAT GOD HAS CHOSEN YOU

FACT:

FASTING WILL GIVE YOU BALANCE

INSPIRATION:

DO WHAT YOU CAN DO AND DO IT WITH STYLE

Destiny Come Forth

November 16

PRAYER:

MAY YOU TAKE HOLD OF YOUR FUTURE

MAY YOU WALK RIGHT INTO GOD'S PROMISES

MAY YOU BE A HOLY LIGHT

MAY YOU BE FUN AND PEACEFUL

MAY YOU DISPLAY GOD'S LOVE

AMEN

DECREE:

THE JOY OF THE LORD BELONGS TO YOU

YOU ARE FULL OF FUN

YOU BLESS EVERYONE ON YOUR PATH

YOU ARE ALWAYS UP FOR AN ADVENTURE

YOU TRY TO ENJOY EVERY DAY

AMEN

FACT:

FASTING PARTNERS WITH FAITH

INSPIRATION:

LET GOD MOVE RIGHT THROUGH YOU

Destiny Come Forth

November 17

PRAYER:

MAY YOU DO FUN THINGS TODAY

MAY YOU REACH UPWARD

MAY YOU KEEP FIRST THINGS FIRST

MAY YOU SEEK GOD

MAY YOU SHARE YOUR HOLY LIFE WITH OTHERS

AMEN

DECREE:

YOU ARE A GREAT ORGANIZER

YOU PLAN ON HAVING FUN

YOU ARE A PIONEER

YOUR GOALS ARE HIGH

YOU DESERVE INNER JOY

FACT:

FASTING BUILDS A PROTECTIVE HEDGE

INSPIRATION:

HEALING IS AVAILABLE

Destiny Come Forth

November 18

PRAYER:

MAY YOU LOVE THOSE AROUND YOU

MAY YOU LOVE YOUR ENEMIES

MAY YOU LOVE YOUR FRIENDS

MAY YOU LOVE YOUR FAMILY

MAY YOU LOVE GOD THE MOST

AMEN

DECREE:

YOU ARE IMPORTANT

YOU TAKE TIME TO RELISH IN GOD'S PRESENCE

YOU ARE SMART

YOU HAVE THE JOY OF THE LORD

YOU NEVER TAKE THINGS TOO SERIOUSLY

FACT:

FASTING BUILDS BRIDGES TO HEAVEN

INSPIRATION:

LOOK FOR JESUS IN EVERYTHING

Destiny Come Forth

November 19

PRAYER:

MAY YOU TRY SOMETHING NEW

MAY YOU FIND YOUR PASSION

MAY YOU FOLLOW YOUR HEART

MAY YOU ACHIEVE ALL THAT MUST BE DONE

MAY YOU FIND WHAT YOU ARE GOOD AT

AMEN

DECREE:

YOU ARE HAPPY

YOU ARE INFORMED

YOU ARE EDUCATED ON THE BIBLE

YOU ARE GOOD ENOUGH

YOU ARE FAMOUS IN HEAVEN

FACT:

FASTING FOLLOWS THROUGH

INSPIRATION:

BE DETERMINED TO LET GOD'S JOY KEEP YOU

Destiny Come Forth

November 20

PRAYER:

MAY YOU BE SURROUNDED BY ANGELS

MAY YOU LISTEN TO GOD

MAY YOU DO WHAT HE SAYS

MAY YOU HEED INSTRUCTION WELL

MAY YOU BREATHE IN GOD'S LIFE

AMEN

DECREE:

YOU ARE ENCOURAGING

YOU ARE GETTING STRONGER AND STRONGER

YOU MELT HEARTS

GOD SWOONS OVER YOU

YOU ARE LOVED MORE THAN YOU UNDERSTAND

FACT:

FASTING GROWS YOUR FAITH DAY BY DAY

INSPIRATION:

ALWAYS TRUST GOD AND YOU WILL NOT FEAR

Destiny Come Forth

November 21

PRAYER:

MAY YOU FIND PEACE

MAY YOU FIND REST

MAY YOU FIND JOY

MAY YOU SEEK WISDOM

MAY YOU RECOGNIZE THE TRUTH

AMEN

DECREE:

YOU ARE TOUGH

YOU ARE ARMED BY GOD

YOU HAVE SUAVE BATTLE SKILLS

YOU KNOW HOW TO WIN

YOU USE YOUR EXPERIENCES WELL

FACT:

FASTING COUNTS

INSPIRATION:

GOD PULLS THE BEST OUT OF PEOPLE

Destiny Come Forth

November 22

PRAYER:

MAY YOU SURROUND YOURSELF WITH GOD'S LOVE

MAY YOU SHARE HIS LOVE WITH YOUR LOVED ONES

MAY YOU FOCUS ON WHAT IS GLORIOUS

MAY YOU STAND STRONG IN YOUR DESTINY

MAY YOU BRING JOY TO THE WORLD

AMEN

DECREE:

YOUR JOY IS INCREASING

YOUR HOPE IS SECURE

MOUNTAINS MOVE FOR YOU

GOD TAKES CARE OF YOU

YOUR FAMILY IS BLESSED

FACT:

FASTING MAKES YOUR DAY BRIGHTER

INSPIRATION:

LOCK ARMS WITH GOD

Destiny Come Forth

November 23

PRAYER:

MAY YOU FIND GOD'S PLANS

MAY YOU KEEP THEM BEFORE YOU

MAY YOU MARCH LOUDLY

MAY YOU SING BOLDLY

MAY YOU DANCE INTO VICTORY

AMEN

DECREE:

YOU ACCEPT THE CHALLENGE BEFORE YOU

YOU ARE WILLING TO GIVE GOD YOUR TIME

YOU TRUST GOD WITH EVERYTHING

YOU KNOW WHAT GOD WANTS FROM YOU

YOU DO IT

FACT:

FASTING MOTIVATES

INSPIRATION:

ANSWER THE CALL OF GOD

Destiny Come Forth

November 24

PRAYER:

MAY YOU SEEK GOD'S FACE

MAY YOU LOOK INTO GOD'S HEART

MAY YOU HOLD BOTH OF GOD'S HANDS

MAY YOU DANCE WITH GOD

MAY YOU CELEBRATE TOGETHER

AMEN

DECREE:

YOU ARE THOUGHTFUL

YOU CONSIDER OTHER PEOPLE'S FEELINGS

YOU WALK GENTLY

YOU ARE CAREFUL

YOU ARE A DIADEM

FACT:

FASTING PUTS THINGS IN ORDER

INSPIRATION:

BE GENTLE ALWAYS

Destiny Come Forth

November 25

PRAYER:

MAY YOU WALK WITH GOD

MAY YOU TALK WITH GOD

MAY YOU SERVE GOD

MAY YOU RECEIVE GOD'S INSTRUCTION

MAY YOU FEEL GOD'S APPRECIATION

AMEN

DECREE:

GOD SPEAKS TO YOU

YOU SIT DOWN AND LISTEN

YOU GIVE GOD YOUR TIME

YOU GIVE GOD YOUR TALENTS

YOU ASK GOD TO USE YOU

FACT:

FASTING REJOICES

INSPIRATION:

YOU ARE GOING INTO A NEW SEASON THIS SEASON

Destiny Come Forth

November 26

PRAYER:

MAY YOU FOLLOW GOD

MAY YOU SMILE BRIGHT

MAY YOUR TIMING BE RIGHT ON

MAY YOU MOVE WITH CONFIDENCE

MAY YOU GET THINGS DONE TODAY

AMEN

DECREE:

YOU ARE WELL ABLE TO EXPAND

YOU ARE STRONGER THAN BEFORE

YOU HAVE BEEN MADE NEW

YOU ARE MOTIVATED

YOU HAVE BEEN POSITIONED BY GOD

FACT:

FASTING LIFTS GOD UP

INSPIRATION:

IT'S TIME TO LIVE THE GOD LIFE

Destiny Come Forth

November 27

PRAYER:

MAY YOU GO INTO THE HOLIDAY SEASON WITH GREAT JOY

MAY YOUR HEART FEEL CHILDLIKE AGAIN

MAY YOU TAKE IT ALL IN

MAY YOU GO THE EXTRA MILE FOR YOUR LOVED ONES

MAY YOU BE A RICH BLESSING

AMEN

DECREE:

YOU ARE READY FOR THIS DAY

YOU ARE READY FOR THE HOLIDAYS

YOU ARE ORGANIZED

YOU ARE RIGHT ON TRACK

YOUR PRIORITIES ARE IN LINE

FACT:

FASTING HEALS WOUNDS

INSPIRATION:

REACH FOR GOD EVERYDAY

Destiny Come Forth

November 28

PRAYER:

MAY YOU FIND THE GIFTS OF GOD

MAY YOU TREASURE THEM

MAY YOU DISTRIBUTE THEM

MAY YOU UTILIZE THEM

MAY YOU KNOW THAT YOU ARE A GIFT TOO

AMEEN

DECREE:

YOU ARE CHOSEN

GOD AMAZES YOU

YOU ARE HUMBLED BY HIS GENEROSITY

GOD FLOWS THROUGH YOUR LIFE

YOU ARE A HOLY OCEAN

FACT:

FASTING GENERATES GOODNESS

INSPIRATION:

WIND UP

Destiny Come Forth

November 29

PRAYER:

MAY YOUR LIGHT SHINE RIGHT

MAY YOUR COURAGE INCREASE

MAY THE JOY OF THE LORD IMPLODE IN YOUR LIFE

MAY YOUR REWARD BE CONSTANT

MAY YOU WORK WITH GOD FAITHFULLY

AMEN

DECREE:

YOU ARE STURDY

YOU ARE STRONG

YOU ARE DETERMINED

YOU HAVE BEEN TESTED AND YOU HAVE BEEN TRIED

YOU HAVE BEEN FOUND FAITHFUL

FACT:

FASTING ELEVATES YOUR LIFE

INSPIRATION:

SHOOT FOR PEACE WITH EVERYONE

Destiny Come Forth

November 30

PRAYER:

MAY YOU PUT GOD ON THE FOREFRONT

MAY YOU AIM FOR THE LORD'S EXAMPLE

MAY YOU START FRESH TODAY

MAY YOU GIVE EVERYONE A FRESH START

MAY YOU LOOK AT EVERYONE THROUGH GOD'S EYES

AMEN

DECREE:

YOU ARE WALKING OUT YOUR OWN SALVATION

YOU FOCUS ON YOUR OWN PERSONAL GOALS

YOU WORK HARD

YOU MAKE THE NECESSARY ADJUSTMENTS

YOU MAKE CONTINUAL IMPROVEMENTS

FACT:

FASTING STRENGTHENS YOUR CORE

INSPIRATION:

CLOSED DOORS CAN LEAD YOU TO THE OPEN DOORS

Destiny Come Forth

December 1

PRAYER:

MAY YOUR DAY BE JOY FILLED

MAY YOU EMBARK ON A NEW JOURNEY

MAY YOU BE SUSTAINED

MAY YOU BE FULFILLED

MAY YOU KEEP ON MOVING TOWARD GOD

DECREE:

YOU ARE DETERMINED

YOU ARE AN ENCOURAGEMENT TO OTHERS

YOU ARE SPECIAL TO GOD

YOU ARE NEAR TO GOD'S HEART

YOU ARE CAPABLE

FACT:

FASTING DREAMS BIG

INSPIRATION:

PRESS IN TO GOD

Destiny Come Forth

December 2

PRAYER:

MAY YOU MOVE FORWARD WITH CONFIDENCE

MAY YOU STAY MOTIVATED

MAY YOU BREAK HEAVEN OPEN

MAY YOU BE A PIONEER TODAY

MAY YOU SEARCH FOR GOD'S BEST

DECREE:

YOU ARE LEGENDARY

YOU ARE QUOTE WORTHY

GOD SPEAKS THROUGH YOU

YOU PROCLAIM THE TRUTH

YOU ARE BOLD

FACT:

FASTING PURIFIES

INSPIRATION:

BE FILLED WITH UNCONDITIONAL LOVE FOR OTHERS

Destiny Come Forth

December 3

PRAYER

MAY YOU FIND WHAT YOU ARE LOOKING FOR

MAY YOU BROADCAST THE GOOD NEWS

MAY YOU REACH FAR AND WIDE

MAY YOU TRUST GOD FOR MULTIPLICATION

MAY YOU SPEAK YOUR MIND

AMEN

DECREE:

YOU ARE TREASURED

YOU ARE SACRED

YOU ARE MADE PERFECT IN GOD

YOU ARE WORTH DYING FOR

YOU ARE RIGHT WHERE YOU NEED TO BE

FACT:

FASTING OPENS YOUR EARS TO HEAR GOD

INSPIRATION:

DISTRIBUTE GOOD

Destiny Come Forth

December 4

PRAYER:

MAY YOUR DAY BE FILLED WITH LAUGHTER

MAY YOUR HEART BE FULL OF JOY

MAY YOUR SPIRIT BE HIGH

MAY YOUR STRENGTH BE RENEWED

MAY YOU WALK THE WALK AND TALK THE TALK

AMEN

DECREE:

YOU ARE GOING PLACES

YOU GO IN STYLE

THE JOY OF THE LORD SUPERCHARGES YOUR ATMOSPHERE

YOU NEVER GIVE UP

YOU JUST CONTINUE TO LOOK UP

FACT:

FASTING CHANGES THE LEVEL

INSPIRATION:

JESUS SAID TO GO AND DO THE SAME

Destiny Come Forth

December 5

PRAYER:

MAY YOU BELIEVE IN YOURSELF AS MUCH AS GOD BELIEVES IN YOU

MAY YOU WALK WITH POWER

MAY YOU JUMP INTO YOUR MINISTRY

MAY YOUR HEART BE FILLED WITH LOVE

MAY YOU RUN THE RACE TO WIN

AMEN

DECREE:

YOU HAVE STRONG WILL POWER

YOU STAY IN LINE

YOU GUARD YOUR HEART

YOU GIVE OF YOURSELF

YOU HAVE FOUND THE SECURITY OF GOD

FACT:

FASTING SPEEDS YOU UP

INSPIRATION:

DON'T GIVE THE ENEMY CREDIT

Destiny Come Forth

December 6

PRAYER:

MAY YOU SEEK REFUGE IN GOD

MAY YOU BLOOM WHERE YOU ARE PLANTED

MAY YOU FERTILIZE THE SOIL AROUND YOU

MAY YOU SHARE YOUR GRATITUDE

MAY YOU HELP OTHER PEOPLE BLOSSOM

AMEN

DECREE:

YOU ARE LOUD AND CLEAR

YOU HAVE A SOLID MESSAGE

YOU HAVE PINPOINTED YOUR MANDATE

YOU WALK WITH AUTHORITY

YOU GO ABOUT DOING GOOD TO ALL

DECREE:

FASTING REJUVENATES YOUR HOPE

INSPIRATION:

THE FAMILY OF GOD IS CONNECTED

Destiny Come Forth

December 7

PRAYER:

MAY YOU RISE UP ABOVE IT ALL

MAY YOU PUT YOUR PAST BEHIND YOU

MAY YOU GO INTO THIS NEW YEAR WITH NEW GOALS

MAY YOU FIND EVERYTHING THAT GOD HAS FOR YOU

MAY YOU THRIVE AT THE TOP

DECREE:

YOU ARE ALL SET

YOU HAVE BEEN SET UP BY GOD

YOU ARE READY TO SHOW THE WORLD WHO GOD IS

YOUR LIFE IS FLOURISHING

YOU ENJOY GOD'S FINEST

FACT:

FASTING PUSHES THROUGH

INSPIRATION:

THE LORD SPEAKS TO LISTENING SERVANTS

Destiny Come Forth

December 8

PRAYER:

MAY YOUR LIFE BE BRIGHT

MAY YOU SHINE ON

MAY YOU HELP OTHERS SHINE

MAY YOU FIX YOUR EYES ON JESUS

MAY YOU KEEP THEM THERE

AMEN

DECREE:

THE JOY OF THE LORD SUPERSEDES DIFFICULTIES

YOU HAVE SURROUNDED YOURSELF WITH GOOD STEWARDS

EVERYDAY IS A MYSTERY FOR YOU

YOU ARE UP TO THE TASK

YOU RISE UP AND SHINE BRIGHT

FACT:

FASTING BRINGS HEALTH

INSPIRATION:

WALK LIKE JESUS

Destiny Come Forth

December 9

PRAYER:

MAY YOU CLING TO HEAVEN

MAY YOU EXPECT SIGNS AND WONDERS

MAY YOU TAKE GOD AT HIS WORD

MAY YOU TRUST GOD WITH YOUR LIFE

MAY YOU HAVE UNSHAKABLE PEACE

AMEN

DECREE:

YOU ARE GOING STRAIGHT FOR GOD

YOU ARE ON THE RIGHT TEAM

YOU ARE MARCHING IN THE ARMY OF THE LORD

YOU ARE DOING YOUR BEST

GOD HONORS YOU FOR THAT

FACT:

FASTING FIXES YOUR FOCUS

INSPIRATION:

HOLD YOUR HEAD UP

Destiny Come Forth

December 10

PRAYER:

MAY YOU BASK IN GOD'S LOVE

MAY YOU KEEP ON GOING

MAY YOU HELP THOSE AROUND YOU

MAY YOU ENGAGE WITH OTHERS

MAY YOU BE A PART OF YOUR COMMUNITY

AMEN

DECREE:

YOU ARE STRONG

YOU ARE COURAGEOUS

YOU ARE VALUED

YOU ARE WHOLE

YOU ARE PEACEFUL TO BE AROUND

FACT:

FASTING STRENGTHENS YOUR SOUL

INSPIRATION:

EXAMINE YOUR HEART

Destiny Come Forth

December 11

PRAYER:

MAY YOU BE ENGAGED

MAY YOU BE PRESENT

MAY YOU PAY ATTENTION

MAY YOU HOLD STEADY

MAY YOU USE SELF CONTROL

AMEN

DECREE:

YOU ARE JOYFUL

YOU ARE CARE FREE

YOU BUILD PEOPLE UP

YOU DON'T HIDE

YOU ARE BOLD

FACT:

FASTING FINISHES FIRST

INSPIRATION:

FINDING YOUR PLACE IS EASY WITH GOD

Destiny Come Forth

December 12

PRAYER:

MAY YOU DREAM BIGGER

MAY YOU RECEIVE VISION FROM GOD

MAY GOD GUIDE YOU

MAY YOUR VISION BE ENHANCED

MAY YOU DISCOVER YOUR PEOPLE GROUP

DECREE:

YOU ARE INSPIRED

YOU INSPIRE EVERYONE YOU MEET

YOU ARE DRIVEN BY GOD

YOU DELIVER THE GOOD NEWS

YOU DO WHAT GOD ASKS OF YOU

FACT:

FASTING DEVELOPS INNER STRENGTH

INSPIRATION:

GOD REVEALS YOUR DESTINY

Destiny Come Forth

December 13

PRAYER:

MAY YOU LIVE A JUST LIFE

MAY YOU STAY ON GOD'S PATH

MAY YOU KEEP YOUR EYES ON HIM

MAY YOU BLAZE A HOLY TRAIL

MAY YOU PIONEER WITH PASSION

AMEN

DECREE:

YOU ARE NEEDED

YOU ARE JUST

YOU ARE SMART

YOUR LIFE BRINGS SO MUCH JOY

YOU ARE GREAT

FACT:

FASTING FILTERS THE ATMOSPHERE

INSPIRATION:

GOD THINKS YOU'RE THE BEST

Destiny Come Forth

December 14

PRAYER:

MAY YOU LOVE LIKE THERE IS NO TOMORROW

MAY YOU MAKE EVERY MOMENT MATTER

MAY YOU MAKE THE MOST OF YOUR PURPOSE

MAY YOU LET GOD PINPOINT YOUR PRIORITIES

MAY YOU STAY DETERMINED TODAY

AMEN

DECREE:

YOU ARE HELD BY GOD

GOD SQUEEZES YOU TIGHT

YOU ARE WELL KNOWN

YOUR CHARACTER IS SOLID

YOU ARE SWEET TO THE CORE

FACT:

FASTING OPENS YOU UP

INSPIRATION:

THE SUPERNATURAL SHOULD BE NATURAL

Destiny Come Forth

December 15

PRAYER:

MAY YOU KEEP ON GIVING

MAY YOU KEEP ON RECEIVING

MAY YOU STAY CHEER FULL

MAY YOU REFLECT ON WHAT IS GOOD

MAY YOU ENJOY THIS SEASON

AMEN

DECREE:

YOU ARE FIRED UP

YOU ARE FULL OF GOD'S POWER

YOU KEEP GOD'S GOALS BEFORE YOU

YOU PRESS INTO HEAVEN

YOU PRESS ON TOWARD THE MARK OF THE HIGH CALL

FACT:

FASTING SHEDS BURDENS

INSPIRATION:

STAND UNDER GOD

Destiny Come Forth

December 16

PRAYER:

MAY YOU HAVE THE BEST DAY EVER

MAY YOU ENJOY YOURSELF

MAY YOU KEEP CHRIST IN YOUR LIFE

MAY YOU GIVE HOPE TO OTHERS

MAY LOVE ABOUND AROUND YOU

AMEN

DECREE:

YOU ARE GOD'S BELOVED FRIEND

YOU MOTIVATE OTHERS

YOU BECAME A GREAT WITNESS

YOU STAY FOCUSED ON THE PRESENT

YOU ENJOY EVERY MOMENT

FACT:

FASTING PURGES IMPURITIES

INSPIRATION:

STAY TRUE

Destiny Come Forth

December 17

PRAYER:

MAY YOU STAY ON PACE

MAY YOU FIND PEACE

MAY YOU EMBRACE CHANGE

MAY YOU FOLLOW IN GOD'S FOOTSTEPS

MAY YOU RELINQUISH CONTROL

AMEN

DECREE:

YOU ARE STRONG ALL DAY LONG

YOU LIVE A RIGHTEOUS LIFE

YOU ARE A THREAT TO THE ENEMY

YOU ARE NOT AFRAID

YOU ARE TRANQUIL

FACT:

FASTING OPENS CLOSED DOORS

INSPIRATION:

PUSH PAST THE PAIN

Destiny Come Forth

December 18

PRAYER:

MAY YOU FIND PEACE AND JOY

MAY YOU SHARE YOUR HOPE

MAY YOU BRING GOOD NEWS

MAY YOU TRUST GOD COMPLETELY

MAY YOU RISE UP SOLID

AMEN

DECREE:

YOU ENJOY WHAT YOU HAVE

YOU FEEL GRATEFUL

YOU SHARE

YOU GIVE ABOVE AND BEYOND JUST LIKE JESUS

GREAT IS YOUR ETERNAL REWARD

FACT:

FASTING FINDS GOD

INSPIRATION:

STAY ON TOP OF IT

Destiny Come Forth

December 19

PRAYER:

MAY YOU FOCUS ON THE POSITIVE SIDE OF LIFE

MAY YOU POINT OUT THE GOOD NEWS

MAY YOU HEAR WHAT GOD IS SAYING

MAY YOU SPEAK IT OUT BOLDLY

MAY YOU BE HEARD

AMEN

DECREE:

YOU ARE A SPOTLIGHT

YOU SHINE ON WHAT GOD IS DOING

YOU TURN EVERYONE'S ATTENTION TO HIM

YOU ARE PLUGGED IN

THE SCRIPTURES KEEP YOU FULL OF POWER

FACT:

FASTING TAMES THE FLESH

INSPIRATION:

GOD LOVES YOU TODAY AND EVERYDAY

Destiny Come Forth

December 20

PRAYER:

MAY YOU BE FAST ON YOUR FEET

MAY YOU ALWAYS BOUNCE BACK

MAY YOU STAY POSITIVE

MAY YOU FIND HOPE IN GOD

MAY YOU KNOW THAT ALL THINGS WORK OUT

AMEN

DECREE:

YOU ARE A WINNER

YOU COME FROM GREAT BLOODLINES

YOUR BEST SIDE SHOWS THROUGH

YOU STAY HUMBLE

YOU LOVE TO HELP OTHER PEOPLE

FACT:

FASTING UTILIZES GOD'S POWER

INSPIRATION:

FOLLOW GOD'S LEADING SAVES TIME

Destiny Come Forth

December 21

PRAYER:

MAY YOU DREAM ON

MAY YOU KEEP YOUR HEAD STRAIGHT

MAY YOU HOLD STEADY

MAY YOU BE READY FOR BATTLE

MAY YOU FIGHT SMART

AMEN

DECREE:

YOU ARE WELL TRAINED

YOU HAVE THE TECHNIQUES YOU NEED

YOU ARE INCREDIBLE

YOU ARE HELD HIGH

YOU ARE A CHAMPION

FACT:

FASTING GIVES YOU PEACE

INSPIRATION:

FRESH ANOINTING FOR YOU TODAY RIGHT NOW

Destiny Come Forth

December 22

PRAYER:

MAY YOU TRUST GOD'S HEART

MAY YOU BE BLESSED BY ALL

MAY YOU ENJOY THE HOLIDAY

MAY YOU BE PRESENT

MAY YOU FEEL THE LOVE

DECREE:

YOU ARE AN AMAZING PERSON

YOU ARE GREAT TO KNOW

YOU DO FUN THINGS

YOU LIGHTEN UP THE ATMOSPHERE

YOU ARE CHEERY

FACT:

FASTING CALMS THE STORM

INSPIRATION:

PUT GOD FIRST

Destiny Come Forth

December 23

PRAYER:

MAY YOU GIVE GOD YOUR TIME

MAY YOU GIVE GOD YOUR TREASURE

MAY YOU GIVE GOD YOUR TALENTS

MAY YOU RECEIVE YOUR INHERITANCE FROM OUR FATHER

MAY YOU SPEND YOUR MONEY WISELY

DECREE:

YOUR NAME IS IN THE BOOK OF LIFE

YOU LEAD OTHERS WELL

YOU KNOW HOW TO WORSHIP IN THE RAIN

YOU FIGHT FOR WHAT IS RIGHT

YOU ARE TRUSTED

FACT:

FASTING MAKES A FRIEND OF GOD

INSPIRATION:

HEAR WHAT GOD IS SAYING FIRST

Destiny Come Forth

December 24

PRAYER:

MAY YOU SING IN THE SPIRIT

MAY YOU SPEND TIME WITH FAMILY

MAY YOU HOLD FAST TO YOUR CONFESSION

MAY YOU BE PREPARED TO TESTIFY

MAY YOU BLESS THOSE AROUND YOU

DECREE:

YOU ARE EXCITED

YOU ARE READY FOR CHRIST

YOU HAVE PREPARED YOURSELF IN THE QUIET PLACE

YOU ARE A NEW CREATION

YOU ARE SHINING BRIGHT

FACT:

FASTING MAKES HOLIDAYS EVEN BETTER

INSPIRATION:

SHINE LIKE THE STAR IN BETHLEHEM

Destiny Come Forth

December 25

PRAYER:

MAY YOU WELCOME OUR KING

MAY YOU RECOGNIZE HIS GLORY

MAY YOU KNOW THE TRUE MEANING OF CHRISTMAS

MAY YOU CELEBRATE

MAY YOU HAVE JOY

AMEN

DECREE:

YOU ARE MERRY

YOU ARE WHOLESOME

YOU ARE A DIGNITARY

YOU ARE SURROUNDED BY HEAVENLY HOSTS

YOU ARE CHERISHED

FACT:

FASTING BRINGS BLESSING AFTER BLESSING

INSPIRATION:

MARY CHRIST MUST

Destiny Come Forth

December 26

PRAYER:

MAY YOU HEAD INTO THE NEW YEAR FREE AND CLEAR

MAY YOU FIND GOD'S PLAN

MAY YOU FOCUS ON YOUR GOALS

MAY YOU PROSPER AND PERSEVERE

MAY YOU PRESS IN TO WIN

AMEN

DECREE:

YOU ARE HAPPY

YOU ARE NEW

YOU HAVE ANOTHER WHOLE YEAR IN FRONT OF YOU

YOU ARE EXCITED

YOU ENJOY THE GOOD TIMES

FACT:

FASTING HAS THE KEYS

INSPIRATION:

STAY JOY FULL

Destiny Come Forth

December 27

PRAYER:

MAY THE LOVE OF GOD HEAL YOU

MAY THE LOVE OF GOD HELP YOU

MAY THE LOVE OF GOD RESTORE YOU

MAY THE LOVE OF GOD REBUILD YOU

MAY THE LOVE OF GOD GIVE YOU HOPE

AMEN

DECREE:

YOU CAN DO IT

YOU EXPECT THE BEST

GOD PROVIDES FOR YOU

YOU ARE FEARLESS

YOU DON'T HAVE TO PRETEND

AMEN

FACT:

FASTING STRENGTHENS YOUR HEART

INSPIRATION:

YOU ARE LOVED WITH THE GREATEST LOVE

Destiny Come Forth

December 28

PRAYER:

MAY YOU KNOW WHO YOU ARE

MAY YOU KNOW HOW MUCH YOU ARE LOVED

MAY YOU FEEL APPRECIATED

MAY YOU THINK POSITIVE

MAY YOU GIVE EVERYONE THE BENEFIT OF THE DOUBT

AMEN

DECREE:

YOU ARE PUMPED UP

YOU ARE SUREFOOTED

YOUR GOALS ARE EXPANDING

YOUR FAITH IS INCREASING

YOUR POTENTIAL IS ESCALATING

FACT:

FASTING WORKS FAST

INSPIRATION:

GO INTO THE NEW YEAR WHOLE

Destiny Come Forth

December 29

PRAYER:

MAY YOU REJOICE WITH GOD

MAY YOU TAP INTO HEAVENS SONG

MAY YOU SING WITH ALL OF YOUR STRENGTH

MAY JOY INVADE YOUR ATMOSPHERE

MAY YOU BE STRENGTHENED ALWAYS

AMEN

DECREE:

YOU GRAB THIS NEW YEAR BY THE HORNS

YOU MAP OUT NEW GOALS

YOU ARE CONFIDENT

YOU ARE READY

YOU ARE FULL OF NEW HOPE

FACT:

FASTING FINISHES THE YEAR OFF RIGHT

INSPIRATION:

GOD WILL FIX IT

HE ALWAYS DOES

Destiny Come Forth

December 30

PRAYER:

MAY YOU HAVE PEACE

MAY YOU HAVE HOPE

MAY YOU HAVE HAPPINESS CHEER

MAY YOU USE YOUR SELF CONTROL

MAY YOU EXPERIENCE GOD'S GOODNESS ALWAYS

DECREE:

YOU ARE A FINISHER

HOW GREAT YOU ARE

YOU ARE GLORIFIED

YOU ARE WORTHY

YOU ARE A PURE JOY

FACT:

FASTING STARTS THE YEAR OFF RIGHT

INSPIRATION:

ASK GOD FOR YOUR HEART'S DESIRE

Destiny Come Forth

December 31

PRAYER:

MAY YOU LINE UP WITH GOD

MAY YOU HEAR GOD CLEARLY

MAY YOU ONLY DO WHAT GOD ASKS OF YOU

MAY YOU FIND YOURSELF IN THE RIGHT PLACE DOING THE RIGHT THINGS

MAY YOU ENJOY EVERY MINUTE OF IT

AMEN

DECREE:

YOU HAVE A WHOLE NEW YEAR AHEAD OF YOU

YOU TAKE GOD SERIOUSLY

GOD TAKES YOU SERIOUSLY

YOU SURROUND YOURSELF WITH HIS PEOPLE

YOU ARE HIS SHEEP

FACT:

FASTING REGULARLY IS A GREAT NEW YEARS RESOLUTION

INSPIRATION:

CONGRATULATIONS

YOU DID IT

NOW DO IT AGAIN

Destiny Come Forth

Piper Lumsden

(989)980-7180

piperlumsdenministry@gmail.com